GEORGIOS A. ANTONOPOULOS
ALEXANDRA HALL
JOANNA LARGE
ANQI SHEN
MICHAEL CRANG
MICHAEL ANDREWS

# FAKE GOODS, REAL MONEY

The counterfeiting business and its
financial management

POLICY PRESS SHORTS RESEARCH

First published in Great Britain in 2018 by

Policy Press
University of Bristol
1-9 Old Park Hill
Bristol
BS2 8BB
UK
t: +44 (0)117 954 5940
pp-info@bristol.ac.uk
www.policypress.co.uk

North America office:
Policy Press
c/o The University of Chicago Press
1427 East 60th Street
Chicago, IL 60637, USA
t: +1 773 702 7700
f: +1 773 702 9756
sales@press.uchicago.edu
www.press.uchicago.edu

British Library Cataloguing in Publication Data
A catalogue record for this book is available from the British Library.

Library of Congress Cataloging-in-Publication Data
A catalog record for this book has been requested.

ISBN 978-1-4473-4696-8 (hardback)
ISBN 978-1-4473-4699-9 (ePub)
ISBN 978-1-4473-4700-2 (Mobi)
ISBN 978-1-4473-4697-5 (ePDF)

The right of Georgios A. Antonopoulos, Alexandra Hall, Joanna Large, Anqi Shen, Michael Crang and Michael Andrews to be identified as authors of this work has been asserted by them in accordance with the Copyright, Designs and Patents Act 1988.

Cover design by Policy Press
Front cover: image kindly supplied by www.alamy.com
Printed and bound in Great Britain by CPI Group (UK) Ltd,
Croydon, CR0 4YY
Policy Press uses environmentally responsible print partners

# Contents

# List of abbreviations

| | |
|---|---|
| EUIPO | European Union Intellectual Property Office |
| HMRC | Her Majesty's Revenue and Customs |
| ICT | Information and communication technology |
| IP | Intellectual property |
| IPO | Intellectual Property Office |
| IPRs | Intellectual property rights |
| ISA | Individual Savings Account |
| JARD | Joint Asset Recovery Database |
| MHRA | Medical and Healthcare Products Regulatory Agency |
| NTS | National Trading Standards |
| OECD | Organisation for Economic Co-operation and Development |
| OEM | Original equipment manufacturer |
| OHIM | Office for Harmonisation in the Internal Market |
| OLAF | European Anti-Fraud Office |
| PICPU | Police Intellectual Property Crime Unit |
| PRC | People's Republic of China |
| TFEU | Treaty on the Functioning of the European Union |
| UNODC | United Nations Office on Drugs and Crime |

# Notes on authors

Georgios A. Antonopoulos is Professor of Criminology at Teesside University.

Alexandra Hall is Senior Lecturer in Criminology at Northumbria University.

Joanna Large is Lecturer in Criminology at the University of Bristol.

Anqi Shen is Professor of Law at Northumbria University.

Michael Crang is Professor of Cultural Geography at Durham University.

Michael Andrews is Head of the National Trading Standards e-Crime Team.

# Acknowledgements

We are grateful to the UK Partnership for Conflict, Crime and Security Research (ESRC/AHRC) for providing the funding for this study (Award reference ES/P001327/1). We would also like to thank our interviewees for their time and valuable accounts, as well as Dr Tristram Riley-Smith for his support in various phases of the research project.

# ONE

# Introduction

"There are two categories for the things that are counterfeited. There is everything and there is anything." (Interview with Police Intellectual Property Crime Unit Officer)

The trade in counterfeit and pirated goods is stated to be one of the fastest-growing businesses in the world (Lin, 2011). The World Trade Organization estimates that 7% of all global commerce is counterfeit (UNODC, 2015). The World Economic Forum goes further, suggesting that in 2015, counterfeiting and piracy equated to 10% of the global trade in merchandise, costing the global economy US$1.77 trillion (World Economic Forum, 2015: 3; see also UNODC, 2015). We must acknowledge that, of course, no one knows the scale of counterfeit trade, and there are problems with the estimates, for example, faked goods being valued as directly losing the value of the originals, which assumes that all purchasers of counterfeits would have bought a full-price original, and, more generally, a reliance on heroic estimates from reputable bodies and a tendency for large estimates to trump smaller ones (Andreas, 2010; see also Intellectual Property Office, 2017). Despite the caveats, it is reasonably safe to accept the international law enforcement agencies' view that the trade in counterfeit and pirated goods is now one of the world's most profitable illicit markets.

Product counterfeiting takes place in a number of dimensions, which include safety-critical and non-safety-critical goods, deceptive and non-deceptive counterfeits, and high- and low-quality fakes. The level of imitation and intellectual property (IP) infringement can also vary from the unauthorised use of a brand name, to the use of intentionally incorrect names and logos that resemble a brand, to the unauthorised sale of a legitimately produced designer product (see Lin, 2011: 5). Indeed, 'counterfeiting' has become a catch-all phrase used to encompass the illicit production and distribution of goods and packaging that infringe intellectual property rights (IPRs). The category includes patents, trademarks and copyrights, as well as poor-quality and fake goods that use 'fake brands' created by the counterfeiters themselves and therefore do not involve IP infringement (Shen, 2017). In some instances, it can be useful to situate the production and distribution of fake goods in their respective legal categories, which include counterfeiting (goods violating a trademark, design rights or patent), piracy (tangible goods violating a copyright), imitations, grey-area products and custom-made copies (Prendergast et al, 2002, cited in Gessler, 2009: 36). This is the focus of this book, though we shall clearly show how other forms of illicit and licit trade become entangled within that ambit – as when counterfeit trade is compounded by customs misdeclaration or plain old smuggling to evade duties, which can also involve original products, and trade-based money laundering for instance.

As the opening quote suggests, the scope of product counterfeiting covers virtually every type of commodity.[1] Statistics on seizures of

[1]  The European Union Intellectual Property Office (EUIPO) identifies 12 categories of counterfeited products: (1) Foodstuff, alcoholic and other beverages; (2) Body care items; (3) Clothing and accessories; (4) Shoes, including parts and accessories; (5) Personal accessories; (6) Mobile phones, including parts and technical accessories; (7) Electrical/electronic and other equipment; (8) CDs/DVDs (Antonopoulos et al, 2011), cassettes and game cartridges; (9) Toys and games, including electronic game consoles

tangible goods suggest burgeoning markets in both non-safety-critical goods, such as jewellery and watches, handbags and luggage, sports goods, clothing, and footwear (Wall and Large, 2010), and safety-critical goods that can pose a significant risk to consumers, including food, alcohol (see Shen and Antonopoulos, 2016; Lord et al, 2017; Shen, 2017), tobacco (Shen et al, 2010), children's toys and games, cosmetics, pharmaceuticals (Hall and Antonopoulos, 2016), pesticides, defence/military equipment (Sullivan and Wilson, 2016), electrical equipment and appliances, and car and aeroplane parts (Yar, 2005). Official knowledge indicates that if we look at the market in fast-moving consumer goods, for instance, then 6.5% of all sports(wear) goods, 7.8% of cosmetics and 12.7% of luggage/handbags sold in the European Union (EU) are in some way counterfeit (Office for Harmonisation in the Internal Market, 2014, 2015).

The seriousness of harms associated with counterfeit products tends to be ignored or underestimated. The International Chamber of Commerce (ICC, 2011: 1) suggests that the infiltration of counterfeit goods in the legal supply chain:

> creates enormous drain on the global economy, crowding out billions in legitimate economic activity and facilitating an "underground economy" that deprives government of revenues for vital public services, forces higher burdens on tax payers, dislocates hundreds of thousands of legitimate jobs and exposes consumers to dangerous and ineffective products.

As we shall show, different modalities of counterfeiting create one or all of these effects. However, it is worth contrasting the popular discourse that it is 'fun' choosing cheap imitations with the number of international cases that highlight the serious health risks associated with counterfeit safety-critical goods. Recent examples include the 45% of

and sporting articles; (10) Tobacco products; (11) Medical products; (12) Other products (eg labels, tags, stickers, packaging material and vehicles, including accessories and parts).

road fatalities in Oman that can be attributed to counterfeit spare parts in 2012 alone (Interpol, 2014) and estimates claiming that the trade in counterfeit, falsified and substandard medicines is responsible for the deaths of up to 1 million people worldwide every year (Southwick, 2013; see also IRACM, 2013; Hall and Antonopoulos, 2016; Hall et al, 2017). It is too simple, though, to divide counterfeiting into that which deceives the consumer and that in which they collude. In the UK, the Home Office estimates the social and economic costs of counterfeiting – which include lost revenue to legitimate business, lost revenue to the exchequer, lost jobs and enforcement costs, including criminal justice costs – at £400 million per annum (Mills et al, 2013). All too clearly, knowledge of such economic costs and social harms depends on a number of contextual variables, such as the reporting and recording of incidents, the level of intensity of law enforcement, and the priorities of various state agencies.

In recognition of the sheer volume of fake goods permeating various markets, regulatory and law enforcement agencies are paying increasing attention to product counterfeiting. However, outside of studies associating the revenue streams of counterfeit markets with the activities of violent groups in conflict,[2] little is known about the everyday financial management of the counterfeit trade. While flows

---

[2]  Counterfeiting has been linked with terrorist and separatist groups in Northern Ireland, Spain and Chechnya, as well as with Hezbollah, Al-Qaeda and ISIS, who are reported to be using the revenue generated from the counterfeiting business as a funding source for conflict (see Union Des Fabricants, 2016). Allegedly, even the North Korean regime has been involved in the counterfeiting and international distribution of cigarettes and currency (see Von Lampe, 2016). In the UK, it has been suggested that the Irish Republican Army (IRA) has been involved in the counterfeiting of CDs, game consoles and designer clothes as a means of buying arms. However, 'it is unknown how much of the money generated by these counterfeiting operations goes to terrorist groups and how much is retained for criminal profits' (EUROPOL, 2013: 2). So, while it is clear that some terror groups do use counterfeit goods to finance themselves, it is not the case that the majority of counterfeit trade is implicated in such financing – despite tendencies in the media and by lobby groups to imply that it is.

of counterfeit goods involved in the trade have been placed under academic and popular scrutiny, the financial mechanisms that enable these flows have largely escaped attention. For instance, Chaudhry and Zimmerman's (2008) conceptual framework does not mention finances in either the trading environment or the kinds of remedial actions undertaken (see also Chaudhry, 2017). This is despite the fact that over the last two decades, official and media discourses have paid increasing attention to 'organised crime' finances in general, often portraying crime-money as a corruptive force, a threat to social life and the stability of national and global financial systems (for a critique, see Van Duyne and Levi, 2005; Reuter, 2013; see also Antonopoulos and Papanicolaou, 2014, 2018).

Yet, these accounts have little to say about the everyday nature and dynamics of 'criminal' investment practices, and research on the financial management of illegal markets and other manifestations of 'organised crime' remains limited. Although considerable work has been done on the disposal of the *proceeds* of crime, global money laundering (Schneider, 2012, 2016) and the financing of terrorism (eg Silke, 2000; Levi, 2010a), little has been done in terms of analysing the individuals, structures and processes involved in the '*preceeds*' of crime (Levi, 2010b: 38; see also Reuter, 1985; Moneyval, 2005; Petrunov, 2011; Kruisbergen et al, 2012; Soudijn and Zhang, 2013). Indeed, as the Head of Europol's Financial Intelligence Unit noted in an event held at the Dutch Ministry of Security and Justice in 2015, 'very little is known about the financial management of organised crime' (Navarrete, 2015). This is surprising given the fact that financing is a horizontal issue for all illicit markets (Hicks, 2015: 1). One exception is the Financing of Organised Crime Project (CSD, 2015), which specifically focused on the processes and structures involved in financial investment and management in the illegal tobacco trade, cocaine market and Value Added Tax (VAT) fraud across European member states (see also Antonopoulos and Hall, 2015; Hall and Antonopoulos, 2017). Another is the relatively sound understanding of finance-related issues in drug markets more generally (see Reuter et al, 1990; Naylor, 2004; Brå, 2007); existing work addresses prices, costs of doing business

(Caulkins et al, 1999, 2009; Moeller, 2012), investments and money laundering. At the other end of the scale, there is good aggregate data on the uses of legitimate trade to enable illicit flows of finance (eg Cobham et al, 2014).

The gap in knowledge about financial management in the counterfeiting business raises various questions: 'What are the various forms and sources of financing in counterfeit markets?'; 'Which financial processes and practices are used by those involved in product counterfeiting?'; 'What (if any) interconnections exist between criminal structures involved in counterfeiting and legitimate businesses or financial institutions?'; 'Do information and communication technologies (ICTs) and e-commerce markets offer enhanced financial opportunities for counterfeiters, and, if so, in what ways?'; and 'How do these online processes interact with physical flows of counterfeit goods?'. Moreover, it raises questions about the role of the nature and forms of the money involved. It asks about the relationship of digital and physical money forms, and different quasi-money forms that might be exchanged. It also picks up from classic theorising about money which emphasises that it serves precisely as an abstract form – with Georg Simmel (2004: 210, 301) arguing in *The philosophy of money* that the meaning of money is confined exclusively to its quantitative sum and that only money is 'free from any quality and exclusively determined by quantity'. Money means only that which it can purchase and dissolves its own traces and origins. This cleansing effect is a sentiment echoed in Paul Stoller's (2002) work on West African crafts commodified and turned into art in New York, where a Muslim trader sells what are, to him, idolatrous images and reinvests the money in paying for more to be made in order to feed his family; for him, 'money has no smell'. Money derived from illicit trades such as counterfeiting clearly walks a tightrope of seeking to lose its origins, of being 'laundered' and itself 'laundering' the gains, yet risking being tainted by its origins – of having a bad smell. We shall show that the forms and kinds of money generated and used have 'social meaning' and not just in legal senses, but in how they are purposed, understood and exchanged (Zelizer, 2011).

This book grapples with these questions. The overall aim is to investigate the techniques of financial management in the counterfeit trade. In doing so, it will suggest that the transnational counterfeit trade is not some 'other economy' run by a separate class of criminal actors, but rather intimately tied to ordinary trade, local criminal entrepreneurs and congeries of actors finding arbitrage opportunities created by shifting goods across consumer markets. Focusing on tangible goods, it addresses the ways in which capital is secured to allow counterfeiting businesses to be initiated and sustained, how entrepreneurs and customers settle payments, the costs of conducting business in the counterfeiting trade, and how profits from the business are spent and invested. The study covers the UK in the broader context of what is a distinctly transnational trade. To map the main physical and financial flows in counterfeit markets, the project focuses on trade with the People's Republic of China (hereafter, China). Not only is China a dominant manufacturing force in the global economy with an advanced export infrastructure, but it is also the major global source of counterfeit items (Intellectual Property Office and Foreign & Commonwealth Office, 2015; see also Chaudhry and Zimmerman, 2008; Lin, 2011). The study explores illicit businesses and financial flows between the UK and China, and how they are implicated in the transnational organisation of the counterfeit trade (see Andreas, 1999).

The book consists of five chapters, including the introduction. Chapter Two provides a general overview of the methods and data used in the study. Chapter Three offers an account of the nature and dynamics of the counterfeiting business. Chapter Four deals with the financial aspects of the trade in counterfeit goods. Chapter Five outlines the main conclusions from the study and suggests some directions for future research in the area of counterfeit goods commerce.

# TWO

# Methodology and fieldwork

This short book is based on the findings from a 12-month interdisciplinary, cross-sector, exploratory project. This brought together a team of academics from the social sciences (criminology and sociology), humanities (geography) and law with practitioners from the National Trading Standards e-Crime Team (NTSeCT). The team provided a range of skills and expertise that benefited the research, including a list of contacts involved in the counterfeit trade and its mitigation. The team was involved in collecting and analysing data on the trade in the UK and China, and the processes and practices involved in its financing.

Recognising the value of different sources of data, the research adopted a mixed-methods approach. The combined expertise of the research team was utilised to incorporate approaches from the social sciences, law and humanities. The involvement of the non-academic project partner from the inception of the research ensured that the research was realistic and relevant beyond academia. The research took place in two phases, which allowed the project to develop iteratively. As we will see in what follows, a staged approach was essential for this kind of exploratory project.

## Phase 1: Review of available literature and content analysis of media sources

The first phase of the research involved a literature review, focused on providing the research team with a better understanding of the complex business models associated with the trade in counterfeit products. Alongside the relatively small body of published academic literature, the review included: (1) research reports by academics, research institutes, governments and national and international law enforcement reports (Europol, Interpol, National Crime Agency, etc): and (2) reports by international organisations (United Nations Office on Drugs and Crime [UNODC] and FATF [Financial Action Task Force]), professional associations and private companies that have been either affected by specific types of counterfeiting (eg British American Tobacco) or commissioned by a client to conduct research on a specific market (eg KPMG). Open sources also included media sources; of particular relevance here were press releases from law enforcement agencies, including Her Majesty's Revenue and Customs (HMRC), the Medical and Healthcare Products Regulatory Agency (MHRA) and National Trading Standards. The advantage of the multilingual team meant that Chinese- and Greek-language documents could also be included. Counterfeiting-related information and statistics in the Chinese literature were obtained in published scholarly work that was gathered from the China National Knowledge Infrastructure (CNKI) – the largest academic database in the Chinese language. This allowed an initial examination of UK–China interconnections in the counterfeit trade. For this study alone, 237 additional publications relevant to the research questions were selected for review.

In addition to CNKI, Google and *baidu* (the most popular Chinese search engine) were searched by using keywords in Chinese for 'counterfeit goods' (*'jia-mao-chan-pin'*), 'counterfeit and inferior (goods)' (*'jia-mao-wei-lie'*)[3] and 'combating product counterfeiting'

[3]  In China, 'counterfeit, fake and adulterated goods', pronounced *jia-mao-wei-lie-chan-pin* in Chinese, is a fixed term typically used in legal, official, academic and media discourses.

('*da-ji-jia-mao*') and their variations in order to capture all relevant cases, examples and statistics scattered in open sources. A systematic search of UK and Chinese media databases for stories relating to counterfeiting between 1987 and 2017 provided useful contextual information. As public domain cases, such stories provided reportable illustrations where we might otherwise be bound by confidentiality or legal restrictions. Indicative UK case studies illustrating the financial management of the trade in counterfeit products – including, for example, various forms and sources of financing, relations between illicit structures involved in counterfeiting and legitimate business and financial facilities, and profits in the counterfeit market – were also identified (see, eg, *The Gazette*, 2016; *Yangtse Wanbao*, 2017). Furthermore, this stage of the project allowed the research team to expand their existing contact list of relevant officials and groups that would prove useful in the project's later phases.

## Phase 2: In-depth interviews with knowledgeable actors and ethnographic observations in online and offline sites in the UK and internationally

In-depth interviews were carried out in the UK with law enforcement and other government officials, academics and researchers, criminal entrepreneurs, legitimate entrepreneurs, and other knowledgeable actors. For this phase of the study, participants were identified in four ways. First, during the course of the literature review and media research, specific officials from law enforcement agencies who appeared in reports or media accounts were approached. Second, participants were accessed during the ethnographic fieldwork in counterfeit markets in the UK, Spain, Vietnam and China (see discussion later). Third, a number of potential participants – both officials and criminal entrepreneurs – had already been identified from previous research studies that members of the team had conducted on various manifestations of 'organised crime', including counterfeiting.

In essence, snowball sampling was used as many of our initial participants introduced us to other potential participants. One of the advantages of this method of sampling is the relatively informal way of identifying participants from hard-to-reach populations, such as illegal entrepreneurs (Atkinson and Flint, 2004). Fourth, participants – primarily from the law enforcement side – were suggested by members of the research team affiliated with the NTSeCT, who effectively operated as our 'gatekeepers', and identified during relevant conferences and events on counterfeiting and illicit financing in the UK and Europe.

A total of 31 interviews with participants were conducted. During this phase of the study, the research team's main objective was to develop a sample that could provide informed and detailed accounts of the financial aspects of the trade in counterfeiting. The list of respondents included:

- government and law enforcement officials (eg Intellectual Property Office [IPO], Police Intellectual Property Crime Unit [PICPU], National Trading Standards, NTSeCT, HMRC and MHRA officers);
- Legal business people/representatives (eg international courier companies);
- academics and/or independent researchers;
- experts working in private companies (eg a forensic accountant in KPMG);
- members of international organisations (eg Organisation for Economic Co-operation and Development [OECD], European Union Intellectual Property Office [EUIPO] and Europol); and
- active criminal entrepreneurs specialising in counterfeiting (see Table 2.1).

The introduction to the interview guides used during this phase of the study was identical for all interviewees, though specific modules for the different types of interviewees (experts versus criminal entrepreneurs) were developed. Experts with broader or more general knowledge,

**Table 2.1: Background of interviewees**

| Background | Number of interviewees |
|---|---|
| Government and law enforcement officials | 14 |
| Legal business people/representatives | 2 |
| Academic and independent researchers | 2 |
| Experts/investigators in private companies | 1 |
| Members of international organisations | 3 |
| Active criminal entrepreneurs | 9 |
| Total | 31 |

such as the academics and the forensic accountant, were interviewed on several sections of the schedule, while other interviewees felt comfortable answering only specific questions about the trade and its financial aspects. All questions were open and, depending on the amount of information that a participant could provide, interviews lasted between 20 and 70 minutes.

This phase of the research also involved ethnographic observations across a number of research sites. The research team visited active counterfeit markets in Manchester's Cheetham Hill (Strangeways) area and busy tourist destinations in Spain and across Vietnam and China. Observations were combined with conversations, some of which resulted in accessing suppliers who were willing to be interviewed. Some of these locations are well known for their counterfeit markets, such as Barcelona and the Chinese city of Yiwu – a small city in Zhejiang province known to many as the 'counterfeit capital of China' (Fleming, 2014). Virtual ethnography (VE) was also used to collect some preliminary data online. Although this method is far more effective over a longer time period (see Hall and Antonopoulos, 2016), it was applied here simply to ascertain how the online environment has changed the counterfeit trade, mainly by means of non-participant observation across forums and social media sites in order to analyse existing content publicly available online. This was also useful for gathering information on marketing techniques and prices in the trade.

# THREE

# The nature and dynamics of the counterfeiting business

The counterfeit product supply chain is, like most others, comprising *manufacturing*, *transportation*, *storage* and *distribution/retailing*. According to statistical data supplied by the World Customs Organization, the US Government and the European Commission, most of the world's counterfeit products originate in China. In 2009, China was the source of US$205 million worth of counterfeit goods seized in the US, which was 79% of the value of all counterfeit products seized that year (UNODC, 2010). In 2014, 81% of all intellectual property (IP)-related seizures in the European Union (EU) came from China and another 8% via Hong Kong (Intellectual Property Office and Foreign & Commonwealth Office, 2015), whereas in 2016, China was identified as the country of provenance making up almost 73% of suspected goods infringing intellectual property rights (IPRs) detained at EU borders in terms of value and 66% in terms of volume (Europol and Office for Harmonisation in the Internal Market, 2016; OECD and EUIPO, 2017). Some have attributed this to Confucian cultures of emulation, but such explanations are not really convincing (Cheung, 2009). According to Lin (2011), the manufacturing of counterfeit goods in China is organised regionally. Specific provinces specialise in the production of certain commodities, which are commonly classified as A-, B- or C-level products depending on their quality and distinguishability from genuine goods (Matthews, 2007; Lin, 2011). There is not a simple line, then, for practitioners of legal/illegal, but rather a differentiated categorisation – as can also be seen in media piracy in 'notorious markets' like Nevskii Prospect in St. Petersburg (Sezneva, 2012). It has also been noted that in China, *bai-ban* goods (literally 'blank board', referring to unbranded and unlabelled goods) are produced for further 'production' (Shen, 2017; see also Ye, 2000; Guo, 2002). Cultures of copying form a production 'ecosystem' where designs are taken from the *gongban* ('common bowl') and where competition drives process innovation to find ways of manufacturing similar but thus counterfeit (*shanzhai*) products more cheaply.

The movement of counterfeit products from China to the rest of the world is facilitated by complex networks shipping goods via cargo ships, air and online. As we shall see, some of this is done by 'suitcase traders', who exemplify a 'low end' globalisation that is often associated with 'the developing world', but also includes the sort of UK-based traders described later, in a 'transnational flow of people and goods involving relatively small amounts of capital and informal, often semi-legal or illegal transactions' (Mathews et al, 2014: 218). Simple extrapolations suggest a hundred million items probably pass through Hong Kong airport alone in this manner (Mathews, 2007). Larger-scale operators may share or hire shipping containers, often being charged a small premium for *bai-ban* 'knock-off' goods and a slightly larger one for 'counterfeits' by freight forwarders (Mathews et al, 2014: 225). *Xinhua News* (2016) – China's state-run news agency – reported that in the great export manufacturing centre of the southern province of Guangdong alone, 64 incidents were detected in an eight-month period between January and August 2016, all involving counterfeits that were intended for the overseas markets. This was an increase of 39.1% compared to the previous year. The confiscated illicit goods were largely shoes, clothing and electricals. Earlier, counterfeiting cases detected in Guangdong involved a workshop making fake top-end perfumes for exportation – 5,000 bottles were produced per day and the fakes were exported once every two days (*Nanfang Metropolis Daily*, 2015) – while 1,000 fake branded mattresses were seized (*Customs Today*, 2015), which add to the previous seizures in 2014 of counterfeit Louis Vuitton luxury items (a much-copied brand to which we shall return later), including 180,000 purses and handbags, 11,000 suitcases, and 30 million fake labels to be applied later and elsewhere to *bai-ban* goods (*Epoch Times*, 2014). The reports lack fine detail, but these high-profile cases indicate the frequency and scale of counterfeit goods exported from the country.

In 2014/15, the overall number of counterfeit products detained at EU external borders increased, despite the drop in caseload. According to Europol and the European Union Intellectual Property Office (Europol and EUIPO, 2017: 12), this:

> indicates the interception of higher unit numbers per case year by year, and is an indication that IPR infringers continue to ship large volume consignments, usually as marine container transport. However, since 2012, the majority of external border seizures have been recorded as postal traffic.

Alongside China, these goods come from counterfeit production hubs in Turkey, Indonesia, Malaysia, Thailand, the Philippines, Ghana, Morocco, Vietnam, Panama, India, Taiwan, Japan and Russia. However, another notable trend observed in recent years is that the manufacturing of fakes has moved to the Global North, including the EU, which also constitutes one of the biggest markets for counterfeit products. Eastern European countries such as Lithuania have been associated with the counterfeiting of alcohol, while Italy and Greece have been associated with the counterfeiting of fashion items. A celebrated example there might be the takeover of fast fashion ('*pronto moda*') in the Italian city of Prato, where some 360 Chinese producers utilise often semi-legal Chinese labour in illicit premises to produce largely legitimate garments but also mix in others that are not 'Made in Italy' (Lan, 2015; Lan and Zhu, 2015). The scale of the trade is such that it has implicated China's largest bank – the Bank of China – in allegedly misdeclared financial flows of €4.5 billion to China from Italy between 2006 and 2010 (Gregson and Crang, 2017). Counterfeit production within the UK is most often of tobacco products. A number of illegal factories have been dismantled by the authorities in various localities such as Grimsby, Glasgow, Aberdeen, Chesterfield and so on over recent years (see also Transcrime, 2013).[4] According to one of our participants, the establishment of counterfeit tobacco factories within the UK has been a response to the low quality of the products manufactured in typical counterfeit-producing countries:

> "Coz they were bringing crap in. Getting bales of crap tobacco from China into Poland and making cigarettes.... They're garbage you know, and the crew asked me to fucking sell them, I said 'No, I'm out of it now, not doing fuck all for us'. I said 'I'm not gonna sell that shit, you know, people don't want them, they're rubbish'." (Interview with criminal entrepreneur #2)

Intra-EU manufacturing involves brand logos being added at the point of sale in an attempt not only to reduce costs associated with production abroad, but also to reduce or eliminate risks in the transportation phase by avoiding inspections by customs at the EU's external borders. Most of the packaging material associated with counterfeit tobacco products, for instance, was stopped at British, Dutch or French borders and was recorded as having originated predominantly from China and Hong Kong (Europol and EUIPO, 2017). Intra-EU processing is not, of course, confined to tobacco products. The so-called '*manteros*' (blanket sellers) of Spanish tourist resorts have been sourcing unbranded consumer goods from warehouses run by Chinese importers in

---

[4] The manufacturing of fake and adulterated products is, of course, nothing new in the UK. During the Second World War, British counterfeiters thrived by producing fake clothing, whereas food and alcohol adulteration with potentially immense consequences was rampant. Two examples involve a consignment of sausages in Hackney, London, containing tuberculous meat and the selling of industrial alcohol that could cause brain damage in West End clubs and bars (Thomas, 2003).

Badalona, a few miles north of Barcelona, and have been adding labels; the networks of factories across Portugal and Spain were estimated to have turned out 235 tonnes of counterfeit clothing and generated €5.5 million in revenues in 2013. How such revenues were recycled to China appears to embroil the world's biggest bank by assets – the Industrial and Commercial Bank of China – whose Madrid branch is now under investigation (*Reuters*, 2017).

The majority of companies producing branded products affected by counterfeiting are registered in the US, France, Italy, Germany, Japan, Switzerland, Luxembourg, the UK (OECD and EUIPO, 2016) and China (Shen, 2017). The UK has been one of the major destination countries for counterfeit products, a trade that has been encouraged by consumer culture and the increased demand for branded products. From 2009 to 2012, for example, the UK experienced a sixfold increase in the number of counterfeit electrical goods seized by the authorities, a phenomenon fuelled by demand for 'branded' designer headphones and gadgets such as hair straighteners. The value of counterfeit electrical goods seized by the authorities at the UK border rose from £2.6 million in 2009 to £15.7 million in 2012, with the value of fake designer headphones rising from just over £200,000 in 2009 to more than £15 million in 2012 (*The Guardian*, 2013). The Organisation for Economic Co-operation and Development (OECD, 2017) suggests that counterfeit information and communication technology (ICT) products account for 6.5% of the total of this type of trade. Similarly, seizures of counterfeit alcohol by the National Trading Standards increased fivefold from 2009 to 2014, and such cases now account for 73% of all investigations by UK trading standards authorities (*The Guardian*, 2014). The research identified socio-economically deprived areas in the UK as hotspots for the sale of counterfeits. Schemes included high-volume/low-value transactions (eg tobacco, alcohol), as well as low-volume/high-value transactions with a small clientele and expensive merchandise (eg watches, jewellery, electronics and highly imitated top-brand vintage wines).

A common perception of supply-side dynamics in counterfeit markets is that the trade is primarily a platform for the activities of centralised criminal structures. Various national and international law enforcement agencies and industry bodies, including the United Nations Office for Drugs and Crime (UNODC), have suggested that increasing links can be found between actors and networks involved in counterfeiting and those involved in arms trafficking, drug trafficking, human trafficking and smuggling, money laundering, and the financing of terrorism. They note the involvement of rigidly structured organised crime groups such as the Russian mafia, Chinese Triads and Italian mafia groups (Union Des Fabricants, 2003). According to the Home Office, 100% of IP theft and counterfeiting in the UK can be attributed to 'organised crime' (Mills et al, 2013). One Home Office study based on 10 in-depth focus groups and a telephone survey of 1,000 randomly selected members of the British public revealed that counterfeiting was one of the forms of crime – along with drug dealing, people smuggling, credit card fraud, extortion, protection, prostitution and paedophile rings – considered to be 'more organised than others' (see also Bullock et al, 2009a: 1). According to Scotland's Serious Organised Crime Strategy, counterfeiting is identified as another type of '*serious* organised crime', and one that includes violence and 'sweatshops staffed by illegal immigrants, students who cannot work and children, who are forced into it' (The Scottish Government, 2016: 8; see also Local Government Association, 2015).

Although the aforementioned perceptions about the nature of the counterfeiting business are partly true for specific geographic contexts, when it comes to the UK, they overlook very important aspects of the counterfeiting business that are integral to our understanding of its characteristics and dynamics. Specifically, some actors may be working in/for 'organised crime groups'; however, most participants in the business are not always manipulated by so-called 'organised criminals' as the official accounts suggest. Individuals involved in the counterfeiting business are often self-employed entrepreneurs. What may be viewed by some as criminal collaboration between a 'producer' and a seller, or a wholesaler and a retailer, does not necessarily involve an employer–employee relationship, but a business-to-business relationship. Individuals are involved in the counterfeiting business via familial, kinship, ethnic and neighbourhood contacts, or via business relationships formed online. An environment of great importance for the formation and consolidation of relationships in the counterfeit trade is legal businesses. Legal businesses also operate as the context in which relationships (employer–employee and between/among partners) are forged and transformed into criminal business relationships (see Von Lampe, 2007; see also Van de Bunt and Kleemans, 2007; Antonopoulos and Hall, 2015).

The research identified different types of product counterfeiting schemes in the UK. *Small-scale schemes* include individuals and networks of actors of Eastern European, Indian and Chinese descent who live in the UK going to their countries of origin for a short period of time and returning to the UK with the merchandise. They also include British holidaymakers and/or professionals who visit typical counterfeit product manufacturing countries and return with various types of fakes (see discussion later). The type and brand of the merchandise bought in these countries to be traded in the UK is not only a case of the potential for profit, but also based on considerations about access to potential customers who would be willing to buy the merchandise. One example from our data is 'Dave', a 36-year-old bartender and part-time English teacher from Liverpool. He has been married to 'Lili' for about four years (interview conducted in April 2017). They met when 'Dave' visited China for the first time with a friend in 2012 to teach English at a summer school for Chinese students planning to study at UK universities. Every summer, he teaches for six weeks in Shanghai, and 'Dave' and 'Lili' stay with 'Lili's' parents and brother in the city. In Shanghai, 'Dave' buys fake TAG Heuer watches for as little as £30 each. His decision to trade in counterfeit TAG Heuer instead of counterfeit Rolex watches is based not on being unable to access the latter brand, but on the fact that his potential clientele would be suspicious of the low price for a Rolex – a commodity that they would find difficult to 'back up' anyway – and thus reluctant to buy:

"The watches are in relatively good condition and they look like the real deal. It's not like we are selling Rolexes for £300 making people suspicious. TAG Heuer are good but not that good, and Joe Bloggs can wear them in the pub or at work. The Rolex ... you have to back it up." (Interview with criminal entrepreneur #4)

Another example from the ethnographic research is that of a UK-based couple that the team observed and interviewed in Vietnam. They buy fake goods (predominantly sportswear, designer handbags, sunglasses and cigarettes) while on biannual holidays in South-east Asia. They have customers who place orders and also sell some merchandise online via Facebook pages:

"We used to go to Europe, now we come to Asia. In Vietnam, knock-off North Face is everywhere and really good quality coz they manufacture the real stuff here. Sportswear, sunglasses, anything Disney for the kids is dirt cheap anywhere in Asia. In Thailand, I have contacts in Phuket who sell me really good-quality designer leather handbags. Mulberry is my customers' favourite now. Some ask for specific designs, others just say get whatever looks good. These are much better than the bags they sell on the market stalls. But they'll set you back 60–100 quid. When we couple that with the amount of cigs that we take back and sell, we can pay for our holidays and then some." (Interview with criminal entrepreneurs #8 and #9)

There appears to be an assumption in counterfeit production countries such as China that foreigners like counterfeit goods. On a recent visit to China, our native Chinese team member, who was accompanied by her English (Western-looking) partner, was approached from time to time by street vendors in several cities, including Shanghai and Guangzhou, and persuaded to buy fake designer bags, sunglasses and watches. It was often said to her that '*lao-wai* [foreigners] all like these', and 'why not buy some and sell them there to get your *lu-fei* [travel money] back?'. Such local beliefs may have some truth, as one Chinese source revealed that the UK market of high-quality counterfeit luxury goods, such as designer handbags, expanded by 60% in 2010/11 (*National Business Daily*, 2015).

*Large-scale schemes* involve the importation of significant quantities (containers, truckloads) of various types of merchandise from China, Eastern Europe (Poland, Ukraine, Russia, Lithuania, etc) and countries in the Middle East. The structure is largely fragmented when it comes to large-scale counterfeiting schemes, that is, a chain of local transactions, though the structure also depends on the type of merchandise produced or smuggled, as well as the scale of the business. A counterfeit tobacco business is generally based on loose networks of entrepreneurs. The trade in more sophisticated products, such as electronics, pharmaceuticals and so on, involves groups that are more centralised, often with a major organising actor who is usually very well connected in other countries (customs intelligence officer #1). The fragmentation of networks involved in large-scale counterfeiting schemes is exemplified by the fact that other members of the counterfeiting networks – even those taking part in a crucial part of the process such as transportation – often know very little or even nothing about the overall scheme (interview with criminal entrepreneur #2).

Even when there is an apparently more sophisticated structure, such as a consortium of entrepreneurs investing money into a counterfeit product importation scheme, there is a middle point in the process represented by lay-bys, industrial estates and other venues in which the presence of lorries is inconspicuous. This is known as a 'slaughter point' in the vernacular of illegal businesses and Her Majesty's Revenue and Customs (HMRC), where the shipment is split and taken to storage locations. From there, the merchandise is transported to the different retail venues managed by *different* and *independent* entrepreneurs.

A large proportion of schemes also operate online and ship smaller packages directly to consumers. This is evident in the remarkable increase in the number of small parcels coming into the UK and corresponding deliveries in recent years:

"When we get a parcel with value £3, £5, £10 or when we come across a Samsung phone or a tablet and on the box the indicative value of the merchandise is £5, it is certainly counterfeit phones and tablets that will be sold in the market for at least £150. These are dangerous devices. We also get hundreds of parcels in the UK with medicines, Viagra or anything else you can imagine really. People do not realise how dangerous this is. And not to mention the counterfeit cigarettes. People send small packages from places like Ukraine, Belarus, China and because it is just a small package, they think we are not going to do anything about it ... we got a package from Hong Kong that read on it that the value of the product was £5. So, two red flags. We opened it and there were about 100–150 MAC lipsticks. These are not produced in sterile environments, and they contain dangerous chemicals. Some smell of petrol, some tobacco, some like shit, literally." (Interview with HMRC officer)

In the counterfeit business (just as in other types of illegal markets), the importance of 'brokers' – actors that bring together two or more disconnected parts of the network – and the service they offer is significant. This is supported by an insider of the trade in China, who claimed that those who run large-scale counterfeiting schemes tend to have their own established distribution channels (*National Business Daily*, 2015). Lin's (2011) study in China found that most counterfeit goods manufactured in China are exported to Taiwanese wholesalers before being redistributed to retailers and customers, not least to try and remove the 'red flags' on suspicious origins. One example from our UK-based research highlights the role played by brokers as they facilitate the entrance of other individuals in different levels of a counterfeiting business:

"Through a friend of a friend, who manufactured cigarettes in Italy and Greece. How I actually got into it was when I moved to Wynyard [a small affluent locality in the north-east of England]. I was already doing fags [cigarettes] before then but on a small scale, but when I moved to Wynyard, I met this chap in the pub at Wynyard. Over the months and months eventually after about a year, he told me he was into cigarettes manufacturing, well, his father manufactured cigarettes in Italy and Greece. He knew what I did, I owned a transport company. Eventually, he said to me, would you think about bringing some cigarettes back?" (Interview with criminal entrepreneur #1)

Other brokers introduce importers (even those involved in small-scale importation schemes) to the right sources of merchandise, which often ensures a certain level of quality (cf Stoller, 2002). 'Dave', the criminal entrepreneur mentioned earlier, for instance, buys 20–30 watches per trip to China. He buys them from a specific tourist shop owned by an old classmate of 'Lili's' brother. 'Lili's' brother, acting as a broker, guarantees that better-quality fakes are procured because of his presence in the trade: "the bloke [Chinese tourist shop owner] sells me better fakes, not the ones sold to tourists" (interview with criminal entrepreneur #4). This was a common theme among entrepreneurs who travel abroad. A local contact can guarantee better-quality fakes at cheaper rates than those sold to tourists by gaining access to 'back-room sellers' who stock higher-quality fakes out of the sight of tourists and the police. In South-east Asia, for example, entrepreneurs spoke of better-quality fakes bought at a higher price, including those branded as 'Mulberry' leather handbags.

Brokerage services can also be offered by people who are actively involved in the trade, such as, for instance, interviewee criminal entrepreneur #5, 'John'. A 58-year-old transportation company owner, 'John' takes care of every detail in his transactions and applies the same principle of diligence in both his legal and illegal businesses.[5] In many cases, brokers facilitate the international transportation of counterfeit products, storage and the provision of the relevant

[5] During the interview, 'John' emphatically mentioned that "mistakes are for losers and amateurs. There is no such thing as a 'coincidence' or bad luck. If you are a professional, no mistakes happen".

documentation to local authorities. The relatively recent collaboration between the Chinese police and the City of London police revealed a case involving a Chinese 'agent' who facilitated the manufacture and distribution of counterfeit clothing and accessories from China to the UK (Europol and Office for Harmonisation in the Internal Market, 2016). Similar findings emerged from our ethnographic observations, which revealed that Chinese individuals now based in the UK send designs and measurements to tailors in China, who then produce and ship the goods back.

Detected cases in China suggest that, more typically, overseas buyers of counterfeit goods place orders for a variety of goods with multiple manufacturers. The goods are then transported to a storage location close to the port before they are placed in containers and shipped abroad (Fu and Hu, 2013). In the international trade, customs clearance is a crucial phase and the process is largely handled, if not monopolised, by the Customs Clearance Agents (CCA) in China. In Yiwu, for example, there were around 3,000 in 2010, some of which were not officially registered. CCAs provide customs clearance services and have a legal duty to inspect the goods that are to be authorised for exportation. In reality, though, often due to cost saving, only paper inspections are conducted. Consequently, illicit goods may be cleared, usually among legitimate exports, to make their way to overseas markets. Given the scale of the problem outlined earlier, it is reasonable to suspect that some CCAs knowingly facilitate the counterfeiting trade at this stage.

The entire transaction may be made through a local agent, or *huo-dai* in Chinese (literally, 'transaction representatives'). *Huo-dai*, formally known as 'forwarder shipping agents', are often native Chinese with a good knowledge of English who work independently or for local international trading companies. As we will see later, 'foreign' nationals (eg British-Irish) who reside in China and speak Chinese also act as brokers in the international counterfeiting trade (Fu and Hu, 2013). According to one *huo-dai* we spoke to, "once goods are cleared, the customs at this [China] side no longer bear responsibilities", and 'it is the overseas buyers who deal with their customs at the other end".

In addition to using local agents, overseas criminal entrepreneurs look for manufacturers of counterfeits at trade fairs and on Internet shopping sites. Some open offices in China and employ local representatives to handle transactions on their behalf (Fu and Hu, 2013). Due to the language barrier, most foreign buyers inevitably hire Chinese–English interpreters.

Criminal entrepreneurs involved in counterfeit markets in the UK are by no means a homogeneous group and many do not meet the archetypal 'criminal entrepreneur' stereotype. Within the aforementioned structures, some entrepreneurs can be seen as *occasional traders*, presented with one-off business opportunities, for instance, on trips abroad. Others could be described as *regulars* who have a different temporal horizon to their business. Criminal entrepreneurs can also be divided into the categories of *specialised* or *versatile* on the basis of the type of merchandise in which they deal. Versatility largely corresponds to the scale of the business, though it is often a result of the restrictions that a local context presents (see Van de Bunt and Kleemans, 2007), for example, huge competition for customers for a specific commodity in a small locality demands diversity. In small-scale schemes, specialisation is the norm, whereas in large-scale schemes, entrepreneurs deal with different types of counterfeit products (perfumes, DVDs, tobacco, alcohol, fashion items, pharmaceuticals) and, in rather rare cases, other illicit commodities such as drugs:

"Some are specialised, some others sell cheap counterfeits of any kind (tobacco, trainers, handbags), some do more than counterfeits. There are cases of drug dealers moving into counterfeits because they want out, they want something slightly more legitimate and less risky. What is better than counterfeits?" (Interview with customs intelligence officer #1)

"There was a particularly noteworthy crime family called the Chaudhry's in Manchester who were actually convicted and ... they were convicted not of drugs trafficking, they were convicted and successfully chased down for their proceeds of crime through the fact that they just couldn't stop being involved in the counterfeiting." (Interview with UK Intellectual Property Office official)

Finally, counterfeiting entrepreneurs have different rationales for entering the business, and interpret 'financial success' in a varied way. For some, participation in the counterfeiting business provides an employment refuge and an antidote to economic exclusion. For such individuals, it is nothing more than a survivalist strategy in 'a desperate search for subsistence income' (Bromley, 2000: 3), often to supplement benefits, whereas for others, it is a means of supplementing legal incomes:

"They are the people who are involved in selling counterfeit goods because they want to make a bit of extra money. They are trying to supplement their income and they're more likely to be in receipt of benefit payments.... That's the nature of the situation, unfortunately, they find themselves in and they're trying to supplement their income or benefit income." (Interview with Police Intellectual Property Crime Unit officer)

"Just a little bit of money on the side, mate ... just a little bit of business every summer, that's all. Simple. Me buying cheap and selling at a higher price back home ... I am a 'one-man band'." (Interview with criminal entrepreneur #4)

For some counterfeiting entrepreneurs – especially among those who have their legal business as the platform for the illegal business – a high 'return on investment' is the crucial rationale for participation: "for some, it's not enough to have some profits. It is not worth it, even though, in counterfeiting, the risk is minimal at best, low at worst. You need to have some significant return on investment" (interview with forensic accountant). High return on investment allows the entrepreneur to invest more in what is perceived to be a promising business venture (legal or illegal) and to attain a position of financial security that can cushion the so-called 'critical moments' of the counterfeiting business.

For other entrepreneurs, the crucial factor is doing better than acquaintances and colleagues involved in the same trade (interview with criminal entrepreneur #2), while for others still, success is when the profit from the counterfeiting business is sufficient to cover for losses in their legal business (most often, transportation companies and retail shops). In the latter case, the counterfeiting business operates as what Skinnari (2010: 207) calls a 'criminal welfare benefits system'. Antonopoulos and Hall (2014) describe these entrepreneurs as 'reluctant criminal undertakers': legal entrepreneurs who are normally involved in the provision of legal commodities/services but dabble in illegal markets within the confines of their legal businesses simply to sustain financial viability.

Finally, for some entrepreneurs, success is not measured in terms of absolute or relative financial success *per se*, but in their very capacity to be seen as 'entrepreneurially inclined' by their immediate social circle. This is especially the case with criminal groups involved in more predatory traditional activities who decide to become involved in counterfeiting (interview with forensic accountant). The activities of this type of counterfeiting entrepreneur resemble one of Antonopoulos and Hall's (2015: 717) participant's accounts of his activities in the illicit tobacco business:

> Hard men from the local community hear about a successful business in the pub and decide that they want to put a little bit of money instead of extort. This makes them feel like 'businessmen', you know, and not like some kind of gorillas.

An important aspect of counterfeiting that is ignored by official, media and business analyses of the phenomenon is the fact that counterfeiting is embedded in legal production and trade practices in a globalised economy. In our research, we came across companies that are geared up to import *legitimate* loads of alcohol and then, at a certain stage in the process, additional counterfeit alcohol shipments in other ports at about the same time and with the same reference numbers. These counterfeit alcohol shipments are called 'shadow shipments':

"There is a ready-made working model. There is no reason to reinvent the wheel. They take advantage of the commerce process, they know what happens in checkpoints, they know there are delays in ports, they know that it is impossible for customs to check all containers." (Interview with HMRC investigative officer)

There are also numerous convergence points between legal, grey and illegal supply chains. Occasionally, a symbiotic relationship develops between the legal and counterfeit supply chains of certain goods. There is, for instance, evidence that counterfeiters have been selling designer knock-offs manufactured by the same craftspeople who produce the originals (UNODC, 2010). This perhaps helps us make sense of some consumer reviews posted on the official website of a high-end fashion brand, such as this one: 'When I first got these the first word that came to mind is "chintzy". If I hadn't have bought them direct, I would have sworn they were a cheap knock off' – this indicates the shift to a new (less-skilled) *legal* manufacturer. The UK system enables open competition, and, as such, counterfeiters are allowed to enter the supply chain more easily because there is less supervision on the part of the authorities (Europol and Office for Harmonisation in the Internal Market, 2016). In the vast majority of cases, counterfeit product manufacturers obtain raw materials from a legitimate material supplier. Counterfeiters often import unbranded commodities, which is not an illegal practice, and, as we saw earlier, attach trademark labels and tags before the commodities are introduced into the retail market. Counterfeiting schemes take advantage of the normal commercial channels (eg postage services, transportation companies or maritime shipping companies that transport containers to the biggest ports around the globe, delivery companies, and so on).[6] Shen et al (2012), in their study of counterfeit tobacco products from China, suggest that there seems to be an identification between the countries that tend to be reported as receptive markets for counterfeit tobacco products and China's top legal trading partners.

Counterfeiting schemes also take advantage of the conducive economic and politico-legal contexts in special economic zones (SEZs), including free zones and export-processing zones. The OECD has identified the abuse of these designated areas as a key facilitator of illicit trade (International Tax and Investment Centre, no date) and they are heavily implicated in the global flow of counterfeit goods. As deregulated conduits designed to attract inward foreign investment, SEZs offer a relatively loose policing and customs infrastructure, as well as lower taxes on imports and exports. Furthermore, sitting 'outside' the standard regulatory structure, they are exempt from the nation-state's laws that govern their geographical location (Hall and Antonopoulos, 2016). As a result, counterfeiting entrepreneurs often make use of SEZs in the production and distribution stages of the supply chain. SEZs used to transit counterfeit products help facilitate the falsification of documents to conceal the original point of departure of the counterfeit merchandise and the repackaging and/or relabelling of the merchandise. Therefore, SEZs are very useful locations for avoiding the interception of merchandise by the authorities at critical points in the distribution process (OECD and EUIPO, 2017).

The EU trade in counterfeit goods is also supported and facilitated by the flow of products created by the *legal* practice of parallel trade. Parallel trade is based on the free movement of trade in the EU internal market and was initially permitted under Articles 28 and 81 of the European Commission Treaty for the Free Movement of Goods and Services within the Internal Market of the EU countries. The legal basis of this trade practice has now been replaced by the Treaty

---

[6] It is interesting to note that the large, international courier firm FedEx was relatively recently indicted in the US on charges of conspiracy to deliver illicit pharmaceuticals (see Walker, 2014).

on the Functioning of the European Union (TFEU), mainly under Article 34: 'It is "parallel" in the sense that it involves products that are essentially similar to products marketed through manufacturers' or original suppliers' distribution networks, but takes place outside (often alongside) those networks' (European Commission Enterprise and Industry, 2010: 23). Parallel trade can be said to be in operation when a product is purchased by a trader in a country where the price is cheaper and, without the authorisation of the owner of the IP rights, exported to another country where the product secures a higher price (see Maskus, 2001). Whereas free trade occurs with the voluntary participation of all parties, parallel trade 'opposes the interests and wishes of the affected manufacturers' (Graham, cited in Wagner, no date: 5). As Hall and Antonopoulos (2016) found in the context of the illicit pharmaceutical business, the UK is one of the largest and most lucrative EU markets targeted by parallel pharmaceutical traders, who legitimately exploit price differentials between states to profit from countries where higher prices result in higher profit margins. However, the permission that the EU gives to parallel trade in pharmaceuticals has had an enabling impact on the trade in illicit medicines in a number of ways, one of which is to provide opportunities for counterfeiters. The process of importing, reimporting, repackaging and reselling provides many opportunities for illicit medicines to enter the legitimate supply chain, offering higher profit margins because the original product will have been bought at a cheaper price. The repackaging process also means that 'pristine packaging is available to be used for counterfeit products, although the redundant packaging is supposed to be destroyed' (Satchwell, 2004: 12). Moreover, trademark owners are prohibited from preventing the repackaging of their products if it is deemed to have no adverse effect on the original manufactured goods (see Laing, 2005: 852; see also Box 1).

## Box 1 Legitimate supply chains, parallel trade, and counterfeit pharmaceuticals

In the summer of 2007, a number of items entered the supply chain as a direct result of parallel trading, including products used to treat psychosis, blood clots and cancer. Some 40,000 packs of tablets were seized by the Medical and Healthcare Products Regulatory Agency (MHRA) and up to a further 10,000 were recalled. Peter Gillespie – whose defence was that he believed he was involved in a legal parallel trade from France – was convicted as the ringleader of a network involved in one of the most serious breaches of the laws that govern the UK pharmaceutical supply chain. In 2011, he was sentenced to eight years in prison and was recently fined £5.6 million. The illicit medicines that he sold were packaged in French but had been produced in China and shipped to Singapore. They were then 'bought by a wholesaler in Luxembourg who sold them on to a Belgian wholesaler and another based in Liverpool, who in turn sold them to UK parallel importers'. This is one of the *known* cases of illegal parallel trade, highlighting the problems associated with a long and complex distribution chain with little regulation opening the EU up to counterfeiters.

*Source*: Hall and Antonopoulos (2016: 86).

Once a shipment arrives in the UK, counterfeiters often use self-storage units to store counterfeit goods before they introduce them into the retail market, and these storage units are rarely monitored by the legal companies operating them (see Europol and Office for Harmonisation in the Internal Market, 2016). In many instances, legal businesses are the sales or use context for the counterfeit products, and are integrally linked to a purely legal service process. Merchandise is very often sold in legal businesses that are related to the legal trade in the commodity (eg counterfeit alcohol being sold in a legal company importing alcohol, eg, a pub):

"When these products go into the normal supply chain, which can happen very often, there can be a situation where, in a supermarket or even a professional, specialist shop for shoes, you buy a counterfeit sports shoe just because the guy, he ordered a certain number of these and he did not pay attention to what the provenance of them was and he gets a part of the shipment of counterfeits. Then the payment methods would be the normal ones – he will pay his supplier in the normal way." (Interview with member of EUIPO)

The following is from a relevant case that we identified in the course of our research: 'Christine' is a 72-year-old hairdresser in a town in the north-east of England. She owns a salon in the transitional zone of the town, and her clientele is primarily older English women and young migrant women. 'Julie' is 28 years old and she is a beautician. She pays 'Christine' a rent of £100 per month to be able to use the premises, as well as have access to the loyal clientele of 'Christine'. 'Julie's' boyfriend, 'Matt', is a truck driver working for an international logistics company doing business with Eastern Europe. Via a Polish partner (known from previous legal jobs) in the city of Łódź, he has identified a group of Chinese businesspeople in the same city. The Chinese trade in a variety of cheap beauty products such as make-up, lipsticks, mascaras and hair products manufactured in China. The merchandise is clearly counterfeit. 'Matt' and his Polish partner buy boxes of beauty products every two months for £2,000 (the money initially came from 'Matt's' savings). Once in the UK, the merchandise is sold by 'Julie' in 'Christine's' salon and/or used by 'Julie' and 'Christine' in their everyday business. 'Christine' does not get involved in the selling of the products, but she enjoys being considered "one of the cheapest hairdressers in [name of the town] and the business has been picking up in these difficult times" (interview with criminal entrepreneur #3). An indicator of the many opportunities for legal businesses to engage in the sale of counterfeit products is offered by Tilley and Hopkins (2008). In their business victimisation survey, 22% of the businesses received offers of counterfeit products on at least a weekly basis, and 20 out of the 420 businesses received such offers at least once a day.

Payments in the counterfeiting business are facilitated by legal service providers and payment gateways, which leads to another important aspect of the counterfeiting business: the increasingly significant role played by ICT. The increase in counterfeit goods being traded has been particularly apparent in the context of various evolutionary phases in technology, with e-commerce now acting as an important avenue through which this criminal market is expanding (see Wall and Large, 2010; Treadwell, 2011; Hall and Antonopoulos, 2016; Large, forthcoming). Technological innovation since the late 20th century has contributed to the trade's mutation to a considerable extent. Internet service providers, registrars, payment processors and payment gateways are increasingly integral legal nodes of the infrastructure needed to trade in counterfeit products. E-commerce facilitates the electronic transfer of money while providing the opportunity to connect suppliers and diversify businesses. Actors who are not necessarily involved in other forms of crime engage in the online trade in counterfeit goods, seeing it as low-risk:

"If you are buying something legitimate on Amazon, for instance, you can sometimes find it's been shipped from Europe, quite legitimately. So that kind of distribution model is a legitimate one. So, of course, it's going to be replicated by criminal elements as well. We've dealt with people before who were buying stuff online, getting it shipped to them and then reselling it on Gumtree or other selling sites or social media sites." (Interview with Police Intellectual Property Crime Unit officer)

"People will ... apply trademarks themselves and what you find, it's not like hardened criminals doing it, just people who go on the Internet and they find guides how to do this and people who are doing this and they think it's okay, so they start their own web page or whatever or Facebook account selling these trainers but they apply like Nike trademarks to it and stuff and Disney and stuff like that.... We had a recent case where a young boy, well it started off with a Gumtree site and he was selling ... Tiffany necklaces that were fake but all this communication was done through What's App and then we passed that information on to Tiff Co ... it turned out it was a 16-year-old boy in Nottingham and when they went to knock on the door, he wasn't there, he was across the country in boarding school and he had got muddled up with an organised crime group somewhere in the UK, we still don't know where, but he'd never met them, he only communicated through What's App, there was no exchange of names or anything like that. It was all just done blankly through What's App and he was running a massive counterfeit Gumtree thing." (Interview with investigator for a private company)

ICTs also provide entrepreneurs with easy access to a significantly higher number of potential customers. Social media sites, particularly Facebook, act as online sites for the supply of counterfeit products. Connections between sellers and buyers are forged via 'friends' lists and Facebook groups affiliated to specific commodities. Stock available is posted directly on individual Facebook walls or on the page of a group, often with photographic evidence of the product alongside personal or business names, contact details, and the date. Virtual 'word of mouth' plays an important role in terms of establishing, assuring and circulating the legitimacy of a seller and the quality of the service on offer, especially as users are concerned about becoming victims of 'scams' and subsequently being defrauded. Some actors use a variety of social networking sites to advertise their products (Hall and Antonopoulos, 2015).

Furthermore, digital technologies limit the opportunities for law enforcement authorities involved in policing the trade:

"The last thing is increasing digitisation of procedures. That, in principle, makes trade more easy and simple and efficient, but, on the other hand, makes customs inspections difficult because there is no human component any more. Two examples – digital forms, digital bills of lading – mean that there's no human interaction between customs and a shipper or an authority. That was a great source of screening. It's great screening when you know with whom you deal. Customs, over time, they were developing this know-how to tell whether you're just one person who deals with legitimate business or whether this is someone who is likely to have something to hide. Another example are these fully automatised customs warehouses where customs have no access, no enter, because boxes move in a fully automated way, which means that even no sniffing dogs can access this. It's great. Boxes go and leave, but there's no inspection and there is a certain cost." (Interview with economist at the OECD)

It is important to note that although there has been a significant shift towards the digitisation of counterfeit markets, there are sub-trends within the online commerce of fakes. In the early 2000s, the biggest issue for authorities was e-commerce sites such as Amazon and eBay. While such e-commerce sites continue to be popular with counterfeiters, social media have now become the dominant online avenue by which people buy and sell counterfeit products in the UK (interview with a National Trading Standards e-Crime Team officer).

# FOUR

# Financial aspects of the counterfeit goods market

## Capital to start and sustain a counterfeiting business

Once a prospective entrepreneur identifies an opportunity to begin supplying counterfeit goods, resources must be mobilised quickly to seize the opportunity. Start-up capital is required for someone to enter the counterfeiting business, cover the costs of establishing the business and operate it until some profit is generated. This initial amount depends largely on the product type and the quantity and quality of the merchandise being traded. There is a wide range of sources that can be drawn upon for the initiation of counterfeiting operations. The first, concerning small-scale schemes, can be *small funds from legitimate work and savings*. This category includes start-up money from social security benefits. This becomes possible because of the extremely low funds that are required for one to enter a counterfeiting scheme selling on a small scale to friends and acquaintances. Ironically, such schemes funded by social security are essentially state-subsidised. Small-scale start-up capital can also include funds from legitimate work and savings, which allows virtually anyone with a small amount of capital to become involved in the business, from holidaymakers to students and those working internationally. The case of 'Dave', the counterfeit TAG Heuer watch entrepreneur, is indicative here. The money invested in his scheme is personal money; savings from his legal work as a bartender from September to June. The amount invested in buying the counterfeit watches is about £900 per year (interview with criminal entrepreneur #4). In another case, we came across a young man living with his parents who operated a Facebook-based business delivering merchandise locally. He started the business by buying £200 worth of counterfeit merchandise from Bristol Fruit Market. The authorities estimated that he made a profit of £20,000 within six months (interview with investigator working in a private company).

Schemes are also funded with *money from legal business*. In this case, the actors are often owners of transportation/logistics companies or legitimate companies trading in the same commodity that is counterfeited (eg alcohol wholesalers trading in counterfeit alcohol). In cases where a scheme becomes successful, it can attract investment from others involved in the trade. Sometimes, the criminal entrepreneurs are presented with opportunities to expand and invite people from their wider social and (legal) business circles to join the scheme. In this way, financing 'consortia' are established with the goal of importing larger loads of better-quality merchandise.

A number of counterfeiting schemes are initiated by *money invested by criminal entrepreneurs*, who branch off into counterfeiting ventures after engaging in other illegal activities. For example, in one case, we came across a cannabis trafficker from Liverpool who invested money from the cannabis business into the counterfeit tobacco business because the risks were extremely low, and because he suspected that the police had become aware of his drugs business. It is also not unusual for criminals to invest small amounts of money into someone else's counterfeiting scheme. This practice tends to be found in small localities in which everyone is familiar with one another and information about successful and profitable illegal schemes flows across social networks. We have found that this is especially the case with counterfeit tobacco (see also Antonopoulos and Hall, 2015) and alcohol schemes. Occasionally, these local criminals extort their way into a counterfeiting scheme in something that could be described as a 'forced investment':

> "I can mention one interesting case with proper criminals dealing in drugs getting involved in extortion, etc, who forced their way into a counterfeiting business. Poor guys selling cheap perfumes all of a sudden paid a visit by a crime group asking them in." (Interview with customs intelligence officer #1)

Some schemes are initiated by counterfeiting entrepreneurs with *loans*. In one of the interviews, the participant was aware of an entrepreneur who had asked for a small loan of £1,500 as start-up capital from his son. In most cases, loans are provided by legitimate businesspeople. We know that loans come with differential interest rates in counterfeiting cases; however, unfortunately, we do not possess any information about the actual rates. Obtaining a loan for a counterfeiting scheme depends, first, on knowing the debtor personally and/or from previous business ventures. The latter is a common occurrence, especially among transportation company owners, who tend to collaborate on international projects, mostly in Eastern and Southern Europe. Legal business owners are more likely to be able to secure a loan and guarantee repayments because:

- their owners tend to be known by the lenders via previous projects or simply as colleagues;
- legal businesses have tangible assets (eg trucks, cranes, premises, furniture, etc) that could possibly be liquidated if there is a difficulty in the loan being repaid. Legal businesses also have a number of intangible but extremely important assets, such as a name and reputation in the business, which, in a way, guarantees some insurance for the lender; and
- legal business owners generally want to avoid the shame of not being able to repay a loan and the repercussions (financial or otherwise) that this has for the borrower in the legal (and illegal) business world (interview with forensic accountant; see also Åkerström, 1985).

In the counterfeiting business, there are two types of 'financiers'. First, there are the ones that are actively involved in other stages of the supply chain, most importantly, distribution/retail markets. Small-scale entrepreneurs are typical of this type of entrepreneur (virtually anyone with a small amount of capital to invest), though some involved in large-scale counterfeiting projects can become involved. For example, in projects we have come across, we found the involvement of consortia of three to five importers who then, in the so-called 'slaughter points', divide the merchandise and sell their parts themselves without any mid-level entrepreneurs or retail distributors being involved. Second, we found some who simply invest in the importation (ie a percentage of the amount required for an importation) and expect a proportionate percentage of the profits after sale. These financiers do not have oversight in any stages of the process, and they tend to be legal entrepreneurs.

Data from Chinese sources seems to suggest an additional 'start-up' scheme. It involves overseas (legitimate and illegitimate) businesses that have unauthorised goods made by Chinese (legitimate and illegitimate) manufacturers on an original equipment manufacturer (OEM) basis. OEM refers to a company that makes parts and products for other companies that sell them under their own name or use them in their own manufacturing. Qian (2008) observed that a large number of private sector labour-intensive enterprises in China have been OEMs for established brand-name products in Japan and developed economies in Europe and North America. Due, in part, to a lack of intellectual property rights (IPR) awareness among private sector manufacturers, especially village and township enterprises, IPR clauses were rarely incorporated in the OEM contracts, and neither had the issue of brand ownership ever been considered. Overseas counterfeiting entrepreneurs who are not genuine brand owners take advantage of this negligence (*Legal Daily*, 2007; Li, 2007; Wang, 2014). Under this scheme, financiers might be legal entrepreneurs and initial production could be jointly funded by the Chinese OEM manufacturer and the overseas entrepreneurs. However, at this stage in the project, we have no firm details about exactly how OEMs are financed.

The counterfeiting entrepreneurs and the investors/financiers are linked in the first instance via the local community and common acquaintances, and are often legal business partners. An investor's share is ensured by trust. This trust is forged primarily in legal business and in previous legal and illegal projects (see Von Lampe and Johansen, 2004). However, in the case of 'forced investment' by an investor or a 'consortium' of investors, the major way in which a share is entrusted is fear of extortion or threat of violence (see Winlow, 2001) from local criminals forcing their way into the scheme.

## Settlement of payments in the counterfeiting business

Usually, small-scale criminal entrepreneurs involved in the counterfeiting business, such as 'Dave', tend to procure merchandise from legal retailers in other countries. Irrespective of the supplier, there are no special arrangements with regards to payment. Cash is almost always given up-front, which is also the arrangement in the transactions between sellers and buyers at the retail level; the basic principle here is 'no money, no merchandise'. Occasionally, if the customer is a good, regular customer with a good record of payments, merchandise is given on credit. In one case discussed by an interviewee, counterfeit fashion items were given to a regular customer who wanted to wear them on his imminent holiday but did not want to spend his holiday money (interview with criminal entrepreneur #5).

At the wholesale/importation level, however, credit may be quite common, especially in cases where the businesspeople involved trust each other and have collaborated in previous legal or illegal projects. The provision of credit is facilitated by the broker, who may be able to vouch for the trustworthiness of the entrepreneur receiving the merchandise on credit. Other criteria of credit provision at the wholesale/importation level include evidence of how 'healthy' the legal business of an entrepreneur is, the presence of collaterals/ assets in the criminal entrepreneur's legal business and evidence that payments (in previous legal and illegal projects) have been delivered on time (interview with forensic accountant). According to

Gambetta (2007: 87), 'the best way to establish one's reputation for trustworthiness is simple: behave well and live up to one's promises'. When a legal business acts as the platform for the counterfeiting business, it becomes a context in which 'good behaviour' and meeting certain financial promises become crucial norms to be manifested and displayed whenever possible. These accounts are largely supported by our observations in China, but the extension of credit appears to be rare in the international trade in counterfeit goods with Chinese suppliers. Payment for a transaction usually starts with a nominal deposit, and the outstanding balance must be paid before the goods leave the port. In this process, agents or local international trading companies act as *de facto* guarantors to ensure that the goods do not leave the country without having been paid for.

When the Internet is used as a medium for the transactions involving counterfeit products, the payments are made either by PayPal or by credit card (interview with member of EU Intellectual Property Office). It is worth noting, however, that the trend among large Facebook sellers based in the UK is that they increasingly prefer to be paid through bank transfers. The reason is that when customers realise that the products they bought online are fake or defective, they cannot claim their money back, as is the case with platforms such as PayPal (interview with investigator in private company). Legal businesses are used as front companies and *existing* payment facilities are used for the sale of counterfeit products. In terms of payments, e-commerce has simplified the process of buying and selling counterfeit goods, but borrowing/renting the bank accounts of friends and family members and setting up offshore banking facilities are also common methods of obscuring the paper trail in the context of online trade in counterfeit merchandise (see Hall and Antonopoulos, 2016). Our observations in China suggest that e-payment via smartphones has now become the most popular payment method in everyday life in urban China, and *zhi-fu-bao* (Alipay) and *wei-xing-zhi-fu* (WeChat Pay) seem to be the most frequently used payment methods in transactions between Chinese suppliers and overseas buyers for both small and large schemes. Similarly, in the UK, as one interviewed academic noted "most of the lads I know involved in selling fakes do it all using What's App, Facebook and PayPal on their phones".

A variety of settlements that do not involve money are also present in a few UK cases. For example, when a batch or a truckload of merchandise is seized by the authorities, usually at the borders, brokers and/or importers require some proof. In this case, those who are responsible for the merchandise when it was seized look for relevant weblinks or for local and/or national newspaper clippings that are scanned and sent electronically to the person who was supposed to receive the merchandise. Similarly, when a package of counterfeit UGG boots was intercepted by Her Majesty's Revenue and Customs (HMRC), the person who was supposed to receive them was sent a letter from the HMRC stating that they had been seized. However, the customer scanned and sent this official letter to the producers and got another pair of boots for free (interview with Europol official). According to a European Union Intellectual Property Office (EUIPO) official: "Some of these guys [counterfeiters] still have a policy of 'If you're not happy, you send it back and I'll reimburse the money'. Some of these guys really have a customer service. They do things very, very well".

In wholesale/importation schemes, a number of people can act as payment facilitators. These are usually people who operate as the brokers who brought together two or more disconnected parts of the scheme in the first place. For example, in importations made in Northern Ireland, people of Irish origin who live and work in China facilitate the payment process between the wholesalers and manufacturers of counterfeit cigarettes in China or the Chinese wholesalers. These Irish brokers have stayed in the country for many years, they speak the language and they have previously conducted business with the Chinese. Financially speaking, it is a simple process: the brokers are paid for their knowledge and local *guanxi* (social networks) in the case of brokers/agents operating in China. They paid towards the upper level (wholesale level) of the business, thousands of pounds per importation, or in the case of large deals, about 1% of the profit made by the UK importer. Unfortunately, because of the fragmented nature of the business and brokers' tendency to operate on the international level, more detailed information is not currently available. What can be said, however, is that in critical moments (eg when a batch is late, seized, lost, etc), the broker who was responsible for bringing together two other parties to conduct business is the first point of contact for both parties and makes sure that frictions of any kind are smoothed over and misunderstandings are cleared. As 'John' – an importer who also acted as a broker for other entrepreneurs – emphatically put it during the interview: "every time a load was lost, seized, late, they busted my balls ... 'Where is it? Where is he? Where are you? Who is going to pay?'" (interview with criminal entrepreneur #5).

Payments between entrepreneurs can be settled outside the strict context of the illegal business, and spill over into the legal side of the business. This tends to be the case with businesspeople who simultaneously do legal and illegal business. Sometimes, when a financial or other settlement cannot be made, where there are delays in the supply of the merchandise, or bad batches, and so on, 'information' becomes a currency in exchanges. This can be information about the legal and illegal dealings of a competitor – which can be potentially interesting and beneficial for the entrepreneur – or another legal or illegal business opportunity, or the possibility of the debtor acting as a broker between the disconnected parties:

> "So, we had the agreement that on such and such day, I will have 350 Louis Vuitton bags. I had already paid the money and told them 'I need the handbags on the day to push forward'. Guess what, the handbags were not delivered in time, my clients were not happy, I was not happy.... The Polish [who the entrepreneur was to buy the stuff from] said 'Sorry boss, here's your money, how can we make it up to you and stuff'. That's not good enough, do you know what I mean ... they said 'OK, do you want to make some money? We will introduce you to our friend who wants to move handmade furniture from Krakow to London. Are we OK?' Not bad, was it?" (Interview with criminal entrepreneur #6)

## Costs in the counterfeiting business

Counterfeiting business costs depend on a variety of factors, which include *the type of counterfeit products manufactured and their quality*. Generally, the quality of counterfeit products varies. Counterfeit alcohol is a good example. In many cases, it is suitable for sale in legal premises (eg corner shops and pubs), but in some other cases, it has been found to be below the required strength. Most counterfeit alcohol poses no threat to consumers' health, but in 2015, an investigation of a pub landlord in County Durham who was selling fake vodka showed that the alcohol contained dangerous ingredients 'used to make antifreeze, disinfectant and fuel' (cited in Lord et al, 2017). The issue here is that some commodities require significant financial investment in the production phase. For instance, making a quality counterfeit microchip (see Kelley, 2012) or a type of pharmaceutical product (Hall and Antonopoulos, 2016) is more expensive than obtaining something like counterfeit raw tobacco.

The Chinese sources were not short of examples that indicate the higher production costs of counterfeit goods made in the country. The process of manufacturing counterfeit perfume involves electric mixers, ingredients (including industrial alcohol, fragrance essences and water), empty bottles and numerous kinds of packaging materials. It cost around 1.3 yuan (£0.15) to make a bottle of fake 'Lancôme' perfume (*China Anti-Counterfeiting Report*, 2016). Similar information is available on other high-profile cases (see, eg, *Nanfang Metropolis Daily*, 2015). In a recent incident detected in Nanjing (*Yangtse Wanbao*, 2017), copies of top-end cosmetics, such as La Mer, Jo Malone and CK (possibly also that handled by Julie, Matt and Christine in the north-east of England, as we saw earlier), were made in plastic buckets stored in a bathroom right next to the toilet, with limited expenses. Thus, the cost of faking a bottle of La Mer moisturising cream could only be several tens of yuan (several pounds in sterling).

By contrast, to make a highly imitated, known as 1:1, Louis Vuitton handbag can be 'costly'. Initial costs include several tens of thousands of yuan (several thousands of pounds) spent on learning techniques and know-how to counterfeit bags. To imitate a top-brand bags involves purchasing a genuine product for around 15,000–25,000 yuan (approximately £1,700–£2,900), taking it apart completely, making patterns and having different parts made by different specialist workshops, and finally assembling and packaging. For a 'mature' counterfeiting business, to 'delicately' copy, say, a Louis Vuitton Limited Edition Love Birds bag would cost around 1,300 yuan (approximately £150). However, making a 'basic' (quality) copy of a Louis Vuitton handbag might cost just over 200 yuan (approximately £23) (*Xinjing Bao*, 2014).

Our research suggests that illicit tobacco factories in Britain, which are specialised primarily in packing tobacco, do not require much investment to yield significant profits. Some entrepreneurs set up their manufacturing business in disused venues. In a case we came across, costs included £200–300 per month for the venue, £5,000 for raw tobacco, £1,000 for counterfeit packs and another £1,000 a month to have a couple of Chinese workers put the tobacco in the packs. In another similar case, the counterfeiters, who set up a tobacco factory in a Grimsby factory, bought the cigarette rolling machine from the Internet (www.AliBaba.com) for £7,000 and paid only £25 per week for the venue. Before the HMRC intervened after only three weeks, the entrepreneurs had made products that guaranteed profits of over £3,000,000 (interview with academic).

Costs also depend on *the scale of the project, its logistical complexity and the level/position on the entrepreneur in the supply chain*. The need for international transactions also significantly affects business costs. Many small-scale entrepreneurs reduce costs by trading a small number of items, using Internet platforms and/or operating their counterfeiting business from their household using spare rooms, garages and basements. The merchandise is stored in their cars, caravans or family members' and friends' houses. Other small-scale entrepreneurs do not have significant costs simply because their counterfeiting trade practices are unsophisticated and embedded in their normal life and work practices. 'Dave', for instance, often pays less than £1,000 for the watches. There are no accommodation costs because he stays with his wife's family in China, and no transportation costs because the merchandise is small, light and easy to carry. His flights from Manchester to Shanghai and back are paid for by the summer school in Shanghai (interview with criminal entrepreneur #4). In some cases, small-scale entrepreneurs reduce the costs of their businesses by sharing expenses with other entrepreneurs. For instance, a venue space divided by stud walls can accommodate six to seven businesses trading, or a small part of a warehouse can be used simultaneously by legal and illegal enterprises. In Manchester, some storage units used by counterfeiters are owned by the City Council (interview with National Trading Standards officer #2; interview with HMRC investigative officer).

However, large-scale operations incur diverse, functional expenses that are unnecessary in small-scale operations. For instance, with no guarantee that a deal will be struck, some counterfeiting entrepreneurs must pay for initial trips to meet with potential partners abroad. Large-scale means bulk; therefore, it can be expensive to transport the merchandise, though these costs will vary according to the distance covered and the risk of seizures or arrests associated with specific UK entry points. However, it is possible for these transportation costs to be significantly different even when the distance covered and the possible risk are identical. For example, according to OLAF (*Office Européen de Lutte Anti-Fraude* [European Anti-Fraud Office]) (2012), in two separate investigations in the UK, one driver received £1,000 per successful Channel crossing and the other received £10,000. Costs associated with 'cover loads' during the transportation of counterfeit products phase should be added (though most cover loads are very inexpensive commodities such as jelly, sand, cattle feed, rotten fruit, etc).

In large-scale schemes, other functional costs include changing the merchandise in containers or moving it from one container to another at ports to confuse the authorities or divert their attention. According to an HMRC source, an average amount paid for this activity is about £250, though it can vary depending on the value of the merchandise and whether the criminal entrepreneurs have done business with the 'movers' before (interview with HMRC investigative officer). In importation/wholesale cases, industrial units (warehouses) are rented to stash the merchandise. In the cases we came across, these industrial units were rented for an average cost of about £50 per month (see also Antonopoulos and Hall, 2015). The security guards working in the premises were given small fees every month to watch and protect the particular units rented by the illegal entrepreneurs:

> "Wholesale is different. You might have to pay up to £10,000 to a lorry driver to transport the cigarettes from France or Belgium or wherever. You need to put the stuff in a warehouse, if you don't want to keep it in your house. You need minders for the warehouse as you are never sure who knows about it and will try to steal it and so on." (Interview with customs intelligence officer)

Large-scale entrepreneurs can also incur higher costs as they attempt to provide better-quality counterfeits in an effort to beat competitors in localities in which counterfeiting thrives. One of the criminal entrepreneurs interviewed ensures high-quality merchandise for his illegal business by mixing high-quality merchandise imported from abroad (Eastern Europe, China and Malaysia) with legally produced merchandise. Occasionally, once every three to four months, they employ burglars to steal bulk quantities of merchandise from legal stores (eg H&M, Debenhams, Topshop, etc) and warehouses where garments are kept. Each entrepreneur employs burglars from their local community to commit burglaries outside the area in which their transportation companies are based. For every burglary, the groups of burglars are paid 30% of the price of the stolen merchandise. The smallest amount paid to the burglars per heist is around £200 and the highest around £3,000, so the cost for this part of the business is roughly £600–£9,000 per year. An additional cost is buying information about warehouses that contain legal merchandise. This information is bought for £200–300 per venue, irrespective of the quantity of merchandise in the premises. The stolen merchandise is sold along with the counterfeit imported items, which facilitates 'counterfeit product laundering' and establishes the entrepreneurs' reputation as merchants of *quality* 'fake' clothes. This quality differentiation is essential if the entrepreneur is to ward off competition from other entrepreneurs operating in the area (interview with criminal entrepreneur #5).

Finally, functional costs include payments to other actors in the counterfeiting business. In our study, we came across payments to *couriers*, individuals who are trusted with transporting merchandise and/or money. Antonopoulos and Hall (2015) refer to a case of the transportation of £1,000,000 of illicit tobacco money from the north of England to someone in London. The courier received £5,000 for the service, or 0.5% of the money transported. On some occasions, legitimate courier companies are used. In September 2014, for instance, three tobacco counterfeiters from the West Midlands were sentenced for their involvement in a counterfeit tobacco smuggling ring. The counterfeiters were arrested by the HMRC, who also seized more than nine tonnes of raw tobacco smuggled in Chinese tea boxes. A search of the home address of one of the entrepreneurs revealed paperwork showing payments made to legitimate courier firms (HMRC, 2014).

Payments are also made to so-called *minders*, people with physical capital who often accompany the money couriers. Unlike couriers, the minders are subcontracted on an ad hoc basis and paid a standard fee per job. Payments must also be made to *retail sellers* who have not invested in a small-scale counterfeiting scheme, but work for someone else. Their daily fee ranges between £20 and £100 (interview with National Trading Standards officer #2; see also Antonopoulos and Hall, 2015). The payments to actors involved in the counterfeiting business can vary widely depending on their role and the size and scope of the operation, as well as the personal relationship between the entrepreneur and the actor. For example, in one of the cases we came across, the entrepreneur used his teenage daughter as his inner-town money courier and did not pay a fee.

Other business costs include *contingency* expenses mostly associated with the risks of losing the merchandise or being found out by the authorities. Although these critical moments can also be experienced by small-scale entrepreneurs, it is mostly large-scale entrepreneurs who tend to incur these costs. For instance, when customs officers find that the cargo manifest is not in accordance with the recorded load, merchandise is confiscated. The HMRC have also come across cases involving batches of counterfeit products (mostly cigarettes and clothes) stolen from warehouses, though the HMRC suggested that the thefts might have been carried out by competitors. Other contingency costs include those related to seizures of vehicles and legal advice following the arrests of criminal entrepreneurs and their associates:

> "The police stopped a van 10 miles from Leeds for a broken windscreen. The officer does a check at the back and he thinks there is something dodgy going on. So, he gives us [HMRC] a call and says 'You might want to take a look at this'. No paperwork.... Turns out it is fake luxury handbags from China." (Interview with HMRC investigative officer)

Finally, costs depend on *the embeddedness of the counterfeiting scheme in a legal business*. Generally, large-scale entrepreneurs who operate within the confines of their legal businesses tend to absorb some of the costs relating to their illegal businesses and the risks associated with them. For example, transportation/logistic companies do not pay for transportation expenses since this is embedded in their everyday business. In addition, they do not have to mobilise human resources for their illegal business. For instance, they do not have to pay workers and drivers, who already work in their legal transportation business and are often unaware of the illegal business taking place:

> "Nothing, they [drivers] always know fuck all, so they get the load and they deliver it to where they're told and they get about two thousand quid ... and then you've got the man, let's say the hinge-pin, over there and he's the one putting the money in anyway, and he'll have contributions from his other pals who help the hinge-pin accumulate the money, so they'll have their costs with running about, distributing, sorting the lorry out and what have you. I don't know how much they've got involved

over there but I was always told the driver never knew. So, I never asked questions, I only wanted to know what I want to know, that's it." (Interview with criminal entrepreneur #2)

In addition, some counterfeiting entrepreneurs who own legal businesses, such as interviewee #5, and who get involved in large-scale counterfeiting schemes have a diverse portfolio (counterfeit tobacco, counterfeit clothes and previously counterfeit alcohol) while operating from a single legal premises. Moreover, international connections and larger investment capability allow them to buy in bulk and get better prices from manufacturers, which creates an economy of scale and a general reduction of overheads. More successful entrepreneurs – and these generally tend to be legal businesspeople – whose initial investments tend to be more substantial, are able to place 'call-off' orders. This basically means that they order a substantial quantity of the merchandise from a producer and take advantage of the usual discount that exists *per single item* ordered and arrange for the merchandise to be sent in instalments to cover demand (interview with forensic accountant).

## Profits and investments in the counterfeiting business

The profit margin in the counterfeiting trade in the UK depends on a number of variables. First, profit margins depend on *whether the entrepreneurs operate within primary or secondary markets.* According to OECD and EUIPO (2016), there are two market segments that counterfeiters target: (1) *primary* markets, in which prices are expected to be close to those of the corresponding products sold in the legitimate market and in which customers are deceived about whether the product is genuine; and (2) *secondary* markets, which involve significant price ranges and customers are expected to pay a much lower price than for the genuine products. Entrepreneurs involved in primary markets tend to make the highest profits, though precise product pricing is a dynamic process in which the counterfeiter uses his/her 'entrepreneurial judgement' (Dean et al, 2010). The art of judgement must take into account: the level of demand for a product and the market potential; the quality of the counterfeited merchandise; the area of sales; the type of clientele and their buying power; competition by other similar entrepreneurs; and the relationship between lowering/reducing prices and the point of maximum profits (see Hotelling, 1929).

Second, profit margins depend on *the position of the illegal entrepreneurs in the supply chain*. The profits begin to reduce as the merchandise moves down the supply chain. Actors in the retail market will make the smallest profit. This is because retailers rely on wholesalers/importers – either by working for them or by buying products from them – and a significant portion of the overall profit is absorbed by actors in this sector of the business. This was observed at Manchester's Cheetham Hill market, where two entrepreneurs spoke of the relatively insignificant role they play as retailers in the supply chain and of the smaller profits that they make as a result:

> "I'm a nobody. These markets are linked to larger networks in Turkey and China." (Interview with criminal entrepreneur #6)

> "The sunglasses are usually £7 but our supplier did us a deal to buy bulk. We still only make £1 per pair if we sell them for £5." (Interview with criminal entrepreneur #7)

Sometimes, the small profit is the result of the retail part of the chain having been extended by 'consumer-retailers', a process that adds layers in the price of the merchandise:

> "When you have a small box, it is most likely going to be resold. Let us say that a box contains 100 lipsticks, sold at a price of £3 each. These will be resold many times and every time, the price will be higher. So the closer you are to the person that receives the package, the lower the price. If you, as the initial customer, buy 10, you pay £30 pounds and then you sell them to your lady friends for £5 each, which is still a good price

and you make £20. Now one of your lady friends might sell a couple for £10 each, also making a few pounds." (Interview with HMRC officer)

Manufacturers and original suppliers also tend to make relatively low profits. The Chinese literature suggests that local manufacturers of counterfeit goods may often only achieve a 2% profit margin from selling their products to overseas importers. The only way to make more is to sell in bulk, while the traders abroad make the highest profits on all amounts (Zhao and Xu, 2009). Third, profits depend upon *relationships between associated businesses/entrepreneurs in a locality*. If business is stable and not severely affected by competition, higher prices can be maintained and the entrepreneurs' return guaranteed (interview with Intellectual Property Office official).

Fourth, *the accessibility of illegal retailers to customers* is an important variable. The use of legal outlets to sell counterfeit products – such as 'Christine's' salon mentioned earlier, or pubs where locals attend and networks are established – seems to increase sales. As 'Dave' noted with regards to his counterfeit watch scheme, within his stable network, "30 watches are sold just like that [flicks fingers]" (interview with criminal entrepreneur #4). In such outlet networks, marketing/promotion occurs organically via word of mouth as the actors' status and reputation within specific locales alerts potential customers to the availability of the merchandise. The longer a counterfeiting operation is in existence, the less the need for advertising as existing customers not only return, but inform new customers by word of mouth. Within this context, merchandise is sometimes sold at a 'discount' or even given free to selected individuals from the entrepreneur's social circle. 'Dave' considers the discounted and/or free watches as "promotional expenses. People might see the watch on one's hand and ask 'Where did you get this from? I want one'. It's good for business and it costs nothing, really" (interview with criminal entrepreneur #4). Occasionally, the discount is created by the entrepreneur by suggesting an *initial* high price for the item (relatively close to the price of the item in the legal market) and then lowering the price significantly.

This incurs no cost to the entrepreneur since the initial high price is *artificially* inflated and does not correspond to the cost of procurement. It also signals product quality, which attracts more buyers. Marketing research has shown that most consumers think that they are buying a better product when they see an initial high price discounted (see Bagwell and Riordan, 1991). Criminal entrepreneurs also sell their merchandise in car boot sales, and increasingly advertise their products on Facebook, Twitter, What's App or Instagram in an effort to expand the circle of potential customers. The Internet and social media not only constitute a 'convergence setting' (Soudijn and Zegers, 2012) for criminal entrepreneurs involved in various parts of the supply chain products, but also facilitate the exchange of information among potential customers (interview with economist at the OECD) and the sales of various commodities to a much broader pool of customers locally, nationally and internationally:

> "The Internet is a formidable market opportunity also for counterfeiters. They use it – there is no doubt about that – but there you have different levels. Some of these Internet sites, as some of the investigators say, sometimes they're even more beautiful than the true ones. They sell the products, and sometimes at quite high prices. They then say, 'We will give you a 10% discount', something like that, and their products are sometimes really of high quality." (Interview with member of EUIPO)

Finally, profits depend on the *time of the year of the sales*. Business and corresponding profits increase significantly at specific times of the year, such as summer and Christmas: "Gets busier at Christmas because there's a lot more of the general public that tend to go down there" (interview with National Trading Standards officer #2).

## Spending and investing profits from counterfeiting

How counterfeiting money is spent and/or invested naturally depends on the profits but also the social microcosm of the entrepreneurs and the opportunities that it offers (Von Lampe, 2007), as well as the entrepreneur's values and priorities. To return to the kind of money involved, we can see in how the profits of counterfeiting are spent the hallmarks of 'special monies'. That is despite how:

> modern money seems starkly homogenous.... Yet camouflaged by the physical anonymity of our dollar bills, modern money is also routinely differentiated, and not just by varying quantities but also by its special diverse qualities. We assign different meanings and designate separate uses for different kinds of monies. (Zelizer, 1989: 342–3)

In many households, money from different sources is designated for different purposes – be that reserving gifted money for special purchases or creating separate funds for particular kinds of discretionary spending, such as an allowance for a hobby. In the same manner, money derived from counterfeiting is often not simply treated the same as all other monies available. Counterfeit trading is often linked to providing the funds for different forms of expenditure, and thus to satisfying specific wants and desires than simply making money for money's sake. It is money with a purpose. We have identified four types of counterfeiting money spending/investing, though there are overlaps between and among different types in many instances.

### Survivalist spending

Survivalist spending is spending the proceeds of small-scale entrepreneurship on essential commodities and services. The entrepreneurs who engage in this type of spending are far away from the 'organised criminal' stereotype. Many engage in the counterfeiting business to supplement benefits and/or low wages.

## *Impulsive/chaotic spending*

Profits from the counterfeiting business are often spent on lifestyle consumption, including luxuries (such as jewellery, antiques, cocaine, expensive cars with high running costs) that allow the conspicuous display of the counterfeiters' success and personal wealth (see Hall et al, 2008): "quite funnily, they [counterfeiters] stick to the areas they come from, disadvantaged areas, and drive expensive cars ... and they wonder why people snitch" (interview with HMRC investigative officer). Ironically, the first thing 'Dave' bought with the money from his first importation of fake watches was a real TAG Heuer Carrera from a major jeweller's chain in the UK: "I could not live with myself knowing that I wear a fake watch". Other purchases include expensive furniture: "We can now say, 'Let's go and buy this handmade coffee table or a dining table with 10 chairs, not six! We even got a king size bed without looking at the price" (interview with criminal entrepreneur #4). Money is also spent on expensive holidays abroad: "Some people [counterfeiters] on Facebook, it's like they're celebrities. 'Oh God, you're in the Maldives again?'" (interview with investigator in private company; see also Junninen, 2006). In one case that involved the importation of six metric tonnes of raw tobacco in hundreds of parcels from Belgium and the Netherlands to the UK, a criminal entrepreneur spent £1.1 million at betting shops in a single year (*The Gazette*, 2016). The couple travelling to South-east Asia spend their profits on the next trip; a rolling investment and return process that pays for their holidays.

## *Family-oriented spending/investment*

Unlike those entrepreneurs who are mostly young with limited social responsibilities and prefer to spend their profits on hedonistic pursuits (see Hall et al, 2008), some entrepreneurs pay off their own and their (extended) family members' debts and mortgages. Others in this category buy or renovate houses and other properties in the UK and abroad (Ireland, Spain or the entrepreneur's country of origin for minority ethnic entrepreneurs) and/or invest in their children's education. Family-oriented spending/investment is usually modest, and, in these cases, entrepreneurs are careful to make sure that it does not extend too far beyond their legal income, thus avoiding too much attention (see also Van Duyne and Levi, 2005; Skinnari, 2010).

## *Business-oriented investment*

Types of business investment are linked to the individual actors' own contacts/networks and areas of previous experience and knowledge (see also L'Hoiry, 2013). For example, we came across an entrepreneur with an existing job in the food supply chain who sought to expand his business using profits from his illicit tobacco business. Actors are typically restricted to investing in areas in which they have some prior experience and expertise.

However, the counterfeiting business itself is also a common target for reinvestment. From the initial moment a scheme becomes successful, part of the profit is invested in subsequent schemes and, occasionally – especially in the case of owners of legal businesses – towards expanding and/or diversifying (see also the previous section). Some criminal entrepreneurs, especially those who are sole entrepreneurs or do not own a legal business that acts as a platform for their counterfeiting business, carefully consider the 'profit–risk' ratio of their business (see Dean et al, 2010). They *deliberately* reinvest relatively small amounts of money (£1,000) and wish not to expand, but simply to maintain a low volume–high value scheme because of the logistical complexities and risks involved in expansion or diversification, which are mostly financial risks that they do not have the capacity to absorb should something go wrong: "Imagine if I brought over 100 watches … I would need a suitcase at least, and what would happen if they are seized at the border? Exactly … my money is gone" (interview with criminal entrepreneur #4).

Similarly, those entrepreneurs with an online component to their business reinvest small amounts from their initial profits in order to maintain a low profile on specific online platforms:

"You just start off with one batch and then you build it up and build it up, but the problem you've got then is if you're on eBay, eBay will make you become a trader, so you will have to put information about yourself on there, so you'd have to hide there, so there are obstacles that you've got to overcome and you've just got to hope that … we're not watching. So, that's another way of doing it, the investment is quite small." (Interview with National Trading Standards officer #3)

Business-oriented investors involve *criminal business*-oriented investors. Although the usual route is for criminals to invest profits from other criminal business into counterfeiting because of the relatively lower risks involved, in one interesting case provided by the HMRC investigative officer we interviewed, a couple invested their profits from counterfeiting and other business activities in the construction of a hotel in Pakistan. It was used as a recruitment and transit point for individuals who were to be trafficked into the UK for labour exploitation:

"We had information about a British Pakistani couple in Bradford. They were owners of a relatively big clothes company in Bradford and our intelligence suggested they were involved in counterfeiting. Clothes, bags, belts, you name it. We raided the premises in this area full of warehouses, and we started searching for money, products, documents. People were also working illegally in the business. One of my colleagues noticed a poster of a big building on the wall. Looked like a big house abroad but the thing is that this house was in bigger and smaller frames in their house too.… In the living room, in the office, in the kitchen. Our investigation revealed that this building was, in fact, a hotel that was built with money from the counterfeiting business and it was used as a recruiting and harbouring venue for trafficked persons from Asia, mostly Pakistan. After they came to the UK, they would work in the clothes company, in restaurants." (Interview with HMRC investigative officer)

## Money laundering

In most UK-based cases, money laundering is unnecessary because criminal entrepreneurs make relatively small profits, perhaps enough to guarantee the entrepreneur and his/her family in the UK or abroad a middle-class quality of life (see Skinnari, 2010).[7] There are, however, large-scale projects in which criminal entrepreneurs need to launder significant profits to remove the specific qualities of the origin of the money and render it indistinguishable from all other money. In a survey conducted by the UK IP Crime Group, 49% of respondents to the UK's trading standards survey indicated that they had worked on cases that involved both counterfeiting and money laundering (UK IP Crime Group, cited in UNODC, no date). In one of these cases, in 2016, a couple from the town of Ballymena in Northern Ireland were sentenced for counterfeiting and money-laundering offences. The couple traded in counterfeit BMW car accessories, making more than £40,000 a month. The prosecutors requested a confiscation of the couple's assets, which had an estimated value of over £1 million (Intellectual Property Office, 2016).

Again, entrepreneurs who own or are in some way involved in a legal business have an advantage over those who do not because they can integrate their counterfeiting proceeds with financial streams in the legal business. For example, as Lord et al (2017) note, the proceeds of alcohol counterfeiting are hidden as an otherwise legitimate business transaction (eg purchases of water), and some profits are laundered via wages to employees. Our research has also identified a diverse set of money-laundering techniques involving investment in payday loan companies. The investment entry level is £100,000 and there is a typical return of approximately 30–40% (interview with HMRC investigative officer). We have also come across investments of counterfeit proceeds in pawn shops or shops that deal in high-value

---

[7]    Although, strictly speaking, such spending may still constitute money laundering pursuant to the Proceeds of Crime Act 2002 (POCA) – the UK's major anti-money-laundering legislation.

items. One of the criminal entrepreneurs interviewed launders money from counterfeiting in illicit puppy farms. He buys Rottweiler and Irish Wolfhound puppies for a relatively low price (£700–800) and sells them at their real/legal market value (£1,200–1,700) (interview with criminal entrepreneur #5). In other cases, counterfeiting entrepreneurs launder money through cash-intensive businesses. For example, in a case we came across, the City of London police identified Turkish counterfeiters who traded in trainers and sportswear, and laundered their proceeds through a cafe, which was also used to physically hide cash in safety deposit boxes.

Profits from the counterfeiting business are also sent via money transfer services from the UK to other countries, mostly in the Middle East, in which a less diligent approach or a lack of knowledge of foreign systems presents barriers to the tracking of criminal proceeds transferred abroad:

"Historically with money service bureaus, it really is a challenge to keep a track because there is so much money flowing, you know, around the world and it can be very difficult to attribute it, you know, we know a lot of cases, we mentioned the Chaudhry's earlier on, this crime family in Manchester. All of their money went to Dubai, where it went from there, I am not too sure. I was out there speaking to a representative of the CPS [Crown Prosecution Service] and she described the Dubai authorities as having a light-touch fiscal approach. When I said 'What does that mean?', she said 'Well, they don't actually give a shit'. Well, that's actually what she said, so, you know, you could effectively turn up in Dubai with a suitcase full of money and if they say 'Well, what are you going to do?', you show them a picture of a flat that you are going to look at and you are going to buy. They are quite happy to let you go and do that because the money then stays in Dubai." (Interview with UK Intellectual Property Office official)

"We tried to track some money back to Dubai accounts, but we couldn't actually reach any further. We have more suspicions as to how this works than actually having the tangible information." (Interview with international courier company representative)

The amounts per transfer seem to average around £2,000 in order to avoid reporting thresholds, though significantly higher amounts are transferred in those cases where counterfeiting entrepreneurs know that they are under investigation by the authorities (interview with HMRC investigative officer; see also Europol Financial Intelligence Group, 2015). Similarly, *Hawala* or *hundi*, an *informal* money transfer system (also known as 'underground banking') (Passas, 2005), has been identified as a means of sending the proceeds of counterfeiting abroad. Based on trust between *hawala* brokers in different countries, a credit with one can be drawn down against the other with the use of a password. This method is popular in cities such as Bradford, Manchester, Birmingham and localities of London, and among British Asian entrepreneurs involved in the counterfeiting business. A major centre of *hawala* brokerage is, indeed, Dubai, which connects remittance flows to the subcontinent, trade-based money-laundering flows from the subcontinent and gold smuggled back into the subcontinent. *Hawala* banking has long been regarded with suspicion, and has been used to rhetorically link counterfeit trades and global terror (De Goede, 2003; Centre for the Analysis of Terrorism, 2016).

The legitimate banking system is also used for low-intensity laundering. An entrepreneur placed small chunks of his counterfeiting profits in a number of Individual Savings Accounts (ISAs). He also transferred profits from one bank account to the other in order to receive the tax-free interest for the amount deposited (interview with private investigator). However, examples of investment in offshore bank accounts are rather atypical cases because most entrepreneurs do not know people who could assist with the practicalities of setting up such accounts (see L'Hoiry, 2013; Antonopoulos and Hall, 2015).

Finally, money laundering is conducted in the guise of donations to charities or aid foundations in the entrepreneurs' countries (interview with National Trading Standards officer #2) and in local mosques in the UK using Muslim business associates to establish links with specific imams (for a similar case in Spain, see also Europol and Office for Harmonisation in the Internal Market, 2016). It should be noted that e-payment systems may also be used for money laundering. However, further research is needed to reveal the extent and impact of this method.

# FIVE

# Conclusion and future directions

This exploratory research has begun to shed light on an area of illicit financing to which academic research has yet to pay much attention. This comes at the same time as international policymakers and law enforcement officials are becoming more concerned about the financial implications of a growing international trade in counterfeit goods. The global market in counterfeit goods is now regarded as the largest illicit market in the world, yet little research has been done to expose its complex dynamics. Indeed, researching and investigating illicit markets and illicit financial flows is a particularly difficult task. The variation in the size and scope of flows, the connection of money to various markets, the lack of cross-sector collaboration, state and business corruption, the transnational characteristic of flows and their spatio-legal differentiation, and the existence of shell companies and offshore entities all present difficult problems for researchers.

As a result of these and other factors, such as time and resource constraints, the current study is limited, but this highlights the need for further interdisciplinary and cross-sector work. For example, there are certain drawbacks to the methodological approach outlined earlier: the short-term nature of the ethnographic observations; reliance on qualitative measures and the opinions of a non-representative sample of interviewees; and the use of data derived from interviews with members of the authorities. The quality of the data from the authorities is dependent upon resource restrictions, the competency of agents, organisational priorities and wider political priorities (see Kinzig, 2004; Levi, 2004; Hobbs and Antonopoulos, 2014). However, while recognising that further in-depth research over a longer time frame is needed, this research, by focusing on the nature and dynamics of illicit financing related to counterfeit markets in the UK and China, has produced some important initial key findings to help illuminate the financial mechanisms and implications of the trade in counterfeit goods. This concluding chapter will summarise the main research findings and offer some possible future directions for further research into the financing of the counterfeit trade.

## Key project findings

The main findings in relation to the financing of counterfeit markets in the UK evidence the relative ease with which actors looking to become involved in the supply of counterfeit goods can find start-up capital to begin a counterfeiting venture, especially for a small-scale project or where capital already exists within a parallel business. In terms of costs, counterfeiting projects do not generally have high sustained business costs. The extent of business costs depends on a range of factors, including the type of goods sold, the quality of goods sold and the scale of the business. Costs can often depend on the extent to which the counterfeiting scheme is embedded in a legal business. Furthermore, the research identified examples which illustrate that not all counterfeiting businesses are of the same size or profit scale. Indeed, many counterfeiting businesses do not make substantial profits. This is not necessarily reflective of the 'success' (or lack thereof) of a business, but is associated with the underlying motivations for and risks associated with the counterfeiting project. Variation of the profit margin is dependent on a number of specific factors, including: whether the trade operates in primary or secondary markets; the position of the criminal entrepreneur in the supply chain; the nature of the locality and local criminogenic structures; the accessibility of counterfeit retailers to customers; and law enforcement pressure in the areas of trading. It is possible to categorise how counterfeiters spend their profits into four broad types: survivalist, impulsive/chaotic, family-oriented and business-oriented.

The research found that in the UK the need for money laundering is limited because of the generally small-scale profit margins associated with most counterfeiting schemes. However, the potential for serious money laundering is to be found, perhaps unsurprisingly, with larger-scale projects where the criminal entrepreneur also has a legal business, which allows for easier integration and 'cleaning up' of criminal proceeds. Where money laundering was part of counterfeiting operations, the research identified a diverse range of techniques, which included money moving through payday loan companies, investments in pawn shops, cash-intensive businesses, profits sent through money transfer services – particularly to the Middle East – and money laundering through the guise of charity or aid foundations.

Importantly, and in line with the growing focus in criminology on cyber-facilitated crimes, the research found that information and communication technologies (ICTs) have transformed the counterfeiting business and its financial management in the UK. The Internet now acts as an important new dimension through which the counterfeit market is expanding. There has been a noticeable increase over the last two decades in counterfeit goods traded in the context of e-commerce markets and social media, with online platforms often acting as a medium for transactions. The Internet, participatory networking and the rapid development of hand-held devices also facilitate communication between and among entrepreneurs, lower the costs associated with advertising and marketing goods, and simplify the process of buying and selling counterfeit goods.

Incorporating research focusing on China as a counterfeit production country, the project has generated a number of important basic preliminary findings that provide a better understanding of the transnational counterfeiting trade and its financial aspects, and that also raise several important questions. The first finding is the crucial role that brokers/agents play in the international trade in counterfeit goods.

The research found that in the case of trading with their counterparts in China, criminal entrepreneurs who are not of Chinese origin tend to rely on local agents for a wide range of services, including language interpretation, negotiations with local entrepreneurs, arranging local transportation, storage and shipping, clearing customs for exportation, and settling payments (this often involves acting as guarantors for overseas buyers). Our data show that large-scale transactions of counterfeit goods between Chinese suppliers and overseas importers are usually made through established business channels, about which we seem to know little, which begs a number of questions: 'How were the networks established?'; 'Who is involved?'; 'How are financial transactions and arrangements made?'; 'Are organisations and individuals within the legal economy's infrastructure, such as insurance companies, accountants and legal advisers, involved in counterfeiting operations?'; and 'How are profits and losses distributed?'.

Second, we find that ICTs have undoubtedly simplified the processes that constitute the transnational counterfeiting business. China enjoys 'late-mover advantages'. The rapid adoption and wide use of e-payment in everyday social life, and in commercial settings (*Financial Times*, 2017; Statista, 2017) from street vendors to much larger businesses, allow payments for literally anything to be made and received in seconds on devices such as smartphones. This may have implications for many financial aspects of the counterfeiting trade, and money laundering in particular, which require further detailed research.

A third striking finding in this study is the involvement of original equipment manufacturers (OEMs) in the transnational counterfeiting trade in relation to China. Existing research is sparse and very little is known about the OEM-initiated counterfeiting schemes in the UK. Thus, further investigation into this type of counterfeiting behaviour and its financing is required.

In addition, the research found some evidence from Chinese sources that indicates an increasing demand for high-quality counterfeits of top-end branded goods in the UK. The level of demand may increase, especially in today's Brexit era, if the pound keeps falling and prices rise. If we experience prolonged economic downturn in the aftermath of the credit crunch, or if there is another similar crash and individuals' spending power shrinks, further demand might increase on a steep curve. This potential trend needs to be closely monitored in future research on product counterfeiting.

Overall, the research found important connections between actors and businesses involved in producing and distributing counterfeit goods in the UK and China. Thus, the findings remind us that while 'counterfeit production countries' in the Global South, and China in particular, are often named and shamed for dumping counterfeit goods onto their 'Northern' neighbours (see, eg, ABC News, 2016; *Forbes*, 2017), we should not forget that counterfeiting is a global trade to which the rules of the market apply. Pang (2008) argued that product piracy is a result of global capitalism rather than the flawed characters of particular individuals or nations, and he thus called to relate the logic of the counterfeit trade to the logic of capitalism itself. At the pragmatic level of policy and practice, although we must have an eye on counterfeiters abroad, we should not ignore 'home-made' criminal entrepreneurs who are motivated to, capable of and active in taking the initiative to place orders for counterfeit products wherever they are available. A principal dynamic at the core of the whole process is consumers' demand for cheap copies of branded goods, a demand constituted and reproduced by late-modern consumer culture (Hall et al, 2008). This is an important point in that it helps us to rethink our anti-counterfeiting policy and strategies and adopt a more rigorous approach to responding to the problems, including deep structural factors in the economy, society and culture associated with counterfeiting practices in the UK – our own jurisdiction, in which policy implementation and enforcement can be (theoretically) guaranteed.

Taking all of the above into consideration, the findings from this research do not seem to support the image of the counterfeiting business as a threatening manifestation of 'organised crime'. Perhaps one could argue that the counterfeiting business highlights that, today, illegal enterprises are no longer 'segregated, morally or physically, from the mainstream of economic society' (Naylor, 1996: 80). Not all schemes are 'organised'; we have come across cases in which merchandise is not delivered on time (while it has been pre-paid), and large schemes having expenses that are not only related to their scale and logistical sophistication, but also related to critical moments that emerge because entrepreneurs rely on others who might not be sufficiently diligent. The idea that a large-scale scheme is 'highly organised' might seem logical. However, the reality of the counterfeiting business is that the larger the scheme, the larger the possible contingencies associated with it. The counterfeit trade is a fragmented business that does not necessarily require a great degree of sophistication and management of finances and resources. Individual entrepreneurs and/or participants in counterfeiting networks are very often opportunists who have identified an opening in the market. In more elaborate schemes, a number of individuals act as intermediaries who bring together disconnected parts (see Morselli and Roy, 2008) by controlling, in a sense, all the informational asymmetries that constitute the networks.

Within the counterfeiting business, there is a wide variety of actors with different personal and social backgrounds, which affect their opportunities for business, the scale of their business, the quality of the merchandise they have access to, the potential clientele they have access to and their spending and investment patterns. Utilising Valenzuela's (2001) typology of entrepreneurship, some entrepreneurs on the retail side of the business can be defined as *disadvantaged survivalist entrepreneurs*, due to their limited employment options at the margins of a stagnating local economy. A number of other counterfeiting entrepreneurs possess skills and resources that are useful and functional for their trade through their legal business and/or employment, and 'for people with a legal commercial business, illegal activities can sometimes become completely interwoven with their daily pattern of activities' (Kleemans and De Poot, 2008: 84). Others depend on personal, social ties, such as *guanxi* (Shen and Antonopoulos, 2016; Shen, 2017) in China, which act as bridges to opportunities for profits, or what Kleemans and De Poot (2008) call 'social opportunity structures'. In addition, these social relations 'solve problems of cooperating in an environment that is dominated by distrust, suspicion and potential deceit' (Van de Bunt and Kleemans, 2007: 173; Von Lampe, 2007). As Van Duyne (2000: 370) notes:

> [c]riminal entrepreneurship is enterprising in an enduring hostile landscape, which means a constant jeopardy of the continuity of the crime-enterprise. For the crime-entrepreneurs it means that the daily organisation of their trade is not only focused on money but at the same time on a highly elaborate risk avoidance strategy. A good crime entrepreneur is an expert risk manager, facing the two-fold close-down by law enforcement as well as by his criminal competitors.

Moreover, our findings do not support the image of crime-money that poses a serious threat to the national and international financial system. Financially speaking, the market in counterfeit products is an attractive market for a number of reasons. It is a potentially large market that covers virtually any legally produced commodity. It is a 'perfectly competitive market' (Makowski and Ostroy, 2001) in the sense that anyone can get involved if they have a small amount of capital to invest. It is low-risk and, unlike markets in drugs and arms, there is an extremely low entry threshold.

As in other illicit markets, importers and wholesalers tend to absorb most costs relating to the business and the risks associated with it (eg the seizure or loss of the merchandise, transportation between/ among countries, etc). As they are primarily situated in the domain of legal business, apart from limiting risks, they have developed relevant expertise and social capital, and they have a range of options for financing a scheme. For instance, a legal business can act as the platform for the easier provision of a loan by other legal entrepreneurs. Simultaneously, when a legal business is the platform for an illegal business, the costs of the illegal business are blended with those of the legal business, for example, premises, storage, transportation, human resources and so on. Finally, these legal businesses are also the terrain upon which payments are often settled, and upon which the provision of credit is facilitated by trust among the actors involved and by brokers who are able to vouch for the trustworthiness of the entrepreneur receiving the merchandise. In a sense, in the counterfeiting business, what one can sometimes observe is the infiltration of the illegal business by the legal business, rather than the other way around.

Most of the entrepreneurs we interviewed, although they manifested entrepreneurial acumen to a varying extent, did not manage profits in a way that was efficient enough to be considered a 'threat' to the social order or the financial system. In fact, the successful management of profits from counterfeiting corresponded to the entrepreneurial acumen of the counterfeiter, the immediate surrounding economy and the entrepreneurs' values and expectations (see Van Duyne, 2007). The entrepreneurs either possessed a small piece of the market with modest profits that simply spilled over into the legal economy, or did not have the capacity to launder bigger profits, perhaps as a direct effect of anti-money-laundering policy and practice (Levi, 2013). It is perhaps the entrepreneurs' low value of assets, coupled with their often chaotic spending patterns, that often results in 'assessed levels of criminal benefits [being] unlikely to be recoverable' and attrition in confiscating the proceeds of crime (Bullock et al, 2009b: 14).

When recognisable money laundering is the case, criminal entrepreneurs are embedded in legitimate businesses, which provide for a very convenient extant setting for this type of financial management (see Kleemans and Van de Bunt, 2008). In these cases, and although there is very little evidence – if any at all – that laundered money from the counterfeiting business constitutes a threat to the national and international financial system and economy, it is plausible to suggest that legal businesses that receive injections of cash and further business opportunities deriving from the trade in counterfeit products may gain an advantage over their legal competitors that are not involved in counterfeiting (or other illicit markets) (see also Spapens, 2017).

The generally unsophisticated financial management practices in the counterfeit products trade are the result of a number of factors, such as the fragmented, decentralised and – as we mentioned earlier – the 'perfectly competitive' nature of this particular trade, which, in the UK, creates an environment where crime-money is widely distributed rather than concentrated in the hands of a few big players. This supports the results of research based on official data on asset confiscation, which shows that although a large amount of organised crime-money exists, and irrespective of the type of asset this money is converted into, its distribution is unequal (see Van Duyne and Soudjin, 2010; Van Duyne et al, 2014). The same seems to apply to many of the counterfeiting entrepreneurs in the UK. According to Bullock et al (2009b), who examined Joint Asset Recovery Database (JARD) data, in 2006/07, 62% of confiscation orders were made for offences of 'drug trafficking', followed by fraud/deception (10% of orders), burglary/theft (7% of orders) and Value Added Tax (VAT) fraud (0.5% of orders). With regards to their value, confiscation orders with the highest *mean* values were VAT frauds (£336,000), followed by money-laundering offences (£255,000), robbery (£21,500), drug trafficking (£20,000) and burglary/theft (£14,500). Counterfeiting did not feature in the analysis precisely because of the relatively low mean value of confiscation orders, which is an indication of the wide distribution of counterfeiting proceeds.

The data from this project, which include observations of active counterfeit markets across the world, including in the UK and China, suggest that despite the 'transnationality' of this illegal market – in as much as it encompasses a multiplicity of interactions and linkages of individuals and institutions across the borders of nation-states – it also has *national* and *local* manifestations that originate in wider economic and social contexts (see Beare, 2000). Our research has shown that the trade in counterfeit products is illustrative of the 'counter-geographies of globalisation' (Sassen, 1998): the dynamic and fluid networks that are to a considerable extent part of the informal economy, but also use sectors of the *legal* economy's infrastructure and social networks across various spatial scales. These networks are intertwined with the foremost dynamics constitutive of globalisation, such as the 'formation of global markets' and the establishment and intensification of 'transnational and trans-local networks', but these are coupled with a diversity of everyday grounded and localised economies (both legal and illicit) and occupational cultures in which the overall process of globalisation is embedded (Sassen, 1998; see also Hobbs, 1998).

## Future directions

There is much more to be done if the complex dynamics of the global market in counterfeit goods and the illicit financial flows associated with it are to be unpacked. This project has identified some specific gaps that require further investigation. For example, future work calls for additional exploration of illicit financing across sites and scales. More can be done to unpack the role of technology in transforming the trade and its financing. Analyses tracing the flows back to accounts situated globally could also tell us more about concentrations of wealth connected to the trade and who is benefiting most. This would take a cross-sector effort involving forensic accountants and the private sector, including the financial services industry. However, privacy laws make this type of research very difficult.

What this study has done is begin to draw attention to the counterfeit goods market as one type of illicit financial flow. To date, there has been too much criminological focus on money laundering and, in socio-legal studies, too much focus on the economic losses of corporate intellectual property (IP) owners. More work is needed on the connection of money to various markets, the mechanisms involved in the connections between micro-finance, wealth management and private banks, and work that takes account of financial innovation, of which there was little knowledge pre-crisis and where legal and regulatory loopholes remain. For example, how are financial derivatives, structured finance (shadow banking practices) and FINTEC (cryptocurrencies) used as facilities for not only money laundering, but also criminal investment practices?

Further research on the policing of counterfeit goods is also important (see Wall and Large, 2010; Shen, 2017). In a time of limited public resources, there is a need for cross-sector information sharing. Whereas this study has managed to collect primary data via ethnographic methods, this is limited to the small-scale actors that we were able to access. However, the purpose should not be to police the trade so heavily that it creates victims and turns public opinion against regulatory, legislative and policing authorities in general (Rojek, 2017). Indeed, there are markets in counterfeits that should be more heavily regulated and policed. Further work should, therefore, aim to inform public policy in the area by extending the mainstream focus beyond the protection of corporate profits to highlight the multiple harms that the trade poses to societies and economies.

Finally, although some evidence in this study suggests a large demand for counterfeit goods in the UK and China, it has not focused on the nature and dynamics of the demand side (for good examples, see Large, 2015, forthcoming; Hall and Antonopoulos, 2016). Lin (2011: 5) offers an important analysis of counterfeiting as a cultural phenomenon, asking 'how counterfeit goods mediate the meaning and value we place on commodities and consumption'. Who decides what is real and what is fake, and where do intellectual property rights (IPR) begin and end? As Rojek (2017) points out, counterfeit commerce, in keeping with all capitalist markets, involves extracting surplus value, which is a dual task accomplished by, on the one hand, driving down the costs of production and, on the other, increasing demand by encouraging the idea that status is gained via ornamental consumerism (see also Hall et al, 2008). Therefore, a critical analysis of the culture of consumer demand and IPR, as they are embedded in the logic of late capitalism, is also important to unpack in future work on counterfeiting.

All of this requires further collaborative research and new research networks at the same time as innovative research techniques (Falzon, 2009; Hall and Winlow, 2015; Hall et al, 2017). The ambition is that this project, by drawing attention to a hugely neglected research area, will be used as an important building block for further research on the culture and economics of counterfeit goods.

# References

ABC News (2016) 'China big in counterfeit goods', *ABC News*, 2 February. Available at: http://abcnews.go.com/WNT/story?id=130381&page=1

Åkerström, M. (1985) *Crooks and squares: Lifestyle of thieves and addicts in comparison to conventional people*, New Brunswick, NJ: Transaction Publishers.

Andreas, P. (1999) 'When policies collide: market reform, market prohibition, and the narcotisation of the Mexican economy', in H.R. Friman and P. Andreas (eds) *The illicit global economy & state power*, Lanham, MD: Rowman & Littlefield, pp 125–141.

Andreas, P. (2010) 'The politics of measuring illicit flows and policy effectiveness', in P. Andreas and K.M. Greenhill (eds) *Sex, drugs, and body counts: The politics of numbers in global crime and conflict*, Ithaca, NY, and London: Cornell University Press, pp 23–45.

Antonopoulos, G.A. and Hall, A. (2015) 'The financial management of the illicit tobacco trade in the United Kingdom', *British Journal of Criminology*, DOI:10.1093/bjc/azv062.

Antonopoulos, G.A. and Hall, S. (2014) 'The death of the legitimate merchant?', in P.C. van Duyne, J. Harvey, G.A. Antonopoulos, A. Maljevic, A. Markovska and J. von Lampe (eds) *Corruption, greed and crime money*, Nijmegen: Wolf Legal Publishers, pp 313–36.

Antonopoulos, G.A. and Papanicolaou, G. (2014) *Unlicensed capitalism, Greek style: Illegal markets and 'organised crime' in Greece*, Nijmegen: Wolf Legal Publishers.

Antonopoulos, G.A. and Papanicolaou, G. (2018) *Organised crime: A very short introduction*, Oxford: Oxford University Press.

Antonopoulos, G.A., Hobbs, D. and Hornsby, R. (2011) 'A soundtrack to (illegal) entrepreneurship: the counterfeit CD/DVD market in a Greek provincial city', *British Journal of Criminology*, 51(5): 804–22.

Atkinson, R. and Flint, J. (2004) 'Snowball sampling', in M.S. Lewis-Beck, A. Bryman and T. Futing Liao (eds) *The Sage encyclopaedia of social science research methods, vol 1*, Thousand Oaks, CA: Sage, pp 1043–4.

Bagwell, K. and Riordan, M.H. (1991) 'High and declining prices signal product quality', *American Economic Review*, 81(1): 224–39.

Beare, M. (2000) 'Structures, strategies and tactics of transnational criminal organisations: critical issues for enforcement', paper presented at the Transnational Crime Conference, Australian Institute of Criminology, Canberra, Australia, 9–10 March.

Brå (2007) *Where did all the Money go?*, Report 2007:4, Stockholm: Brå.

Bromley, R. (2000) 'Street vending and public policy: a global review', *International Journal of Sociology and Social Policy*, 20(1/2): 1–28.

Bullock, K., Chowdhury, R. and Hollings, P. (2009a) *Public concern about organised crime*, Research Report 16, London: Home Office.

Bullock, K., Mann, D., Street, R. and Coxin, C. (2009b) *Examining attrition in confiscating the proceeds of crime*, Research Report 17, London: Home Office.

Caulkins, J.P., Johnson, B., Taylor, A. and Taylor, L. (1999) 'What drug dealers tell us about their costs of doing business', *Journal of Drug Issues*, 29(2): 323–40.

Caulkins, J.P., Gurga, B. and Little, C. (2009) 'Economic analysis of drug transaction "cycles" described by incarcerated UK drug dealers', *Global Crime*, 10(1/2): 94–112.

Center for the Analysis of Terrorism (2016) 'Illicit trade and terrorism financing'. Available at: http://cat-int.org/wp-content/uploads/2017/03/Interim-note-Illicit-trade-and-terrorism-financing-Dec-2016.pdf

Chaudhry, P.E. (ed) (2017) *Handbook of research on counterfeiting and illicit trade*, Cheltenham: Edward Elgar.

Chaudhry, P.E. and Zimmerman, A. (2008) *The economics of counterfeit trade*, Dordrecht: Springer.

Cheung, G.C. (2009) *Intellectual property rights in China: Politics of piracy, trade and protection*, London: Routledge.

*China Anti-Counterfeiting Report* (2016) 'Zhuhai police detected a perfume counterfeiting case', *China Anti-Counterfeiting Report*, 2: 86–7.

Cobham, A., Janský, P. and Prats, A. (2014) *Estimating illicit flows of capital via trade mispricing: A forensic analysis of data on Switzerland*, CGD Working Paper, Washington, DC: Center for Global Development.

CSD (Centre for the Study of Democracy) (2015) *FINOCA*, Sofia: CSD.

*Customs Today* (2015) 'Chinese police seized 1,000 counterfeit mattresses worth \$1.6m', 5 June. Available at: http://www. customstoday.com.pk/chinese-police-seized-1000-counterfeit-mattresses-worth-1-6m-2/

Dean, G., Fahsing, I. and Gottschalk, I. (2010) *Organised crime: Policing illegal business entrepreneurialism*, Oxford: Oxford University Press.

De Goede, M. (2003) 'Hawala discourses and the war on terrorist finance', *Environment and Planning D: Society and Space*, 21(5): 513–32.

*Epoch Times* (2014) 'Counterfeit Louis Vuitton goods worth one billion yuan are seized in Southern China', *Epoch Times*, 18 September. Available at: https://www.theepochtimes.com/counterfeit-louis-vuitton-goods-worth-one-billion-yuan-are-seized-in-southern-china_966058.html

European Commission Enterprise and Industry (2010) *Free movement of goods: Guide to the application of Treaty provisions governing the free movements of goods*, Luxembourg: Publications Office of the European Union.

Europol (2013) *EU serious and organised crime threat assessment*, The Hague: Europol.

Europol Financial Intelligence Group (2015) *Why is cash still king? A strategic report on the use of cash by criminal groups as a facilitator for money laundering*, The Hague: Europol.

Europol and EUIPO (European Union Intellectual Property Office) (2017) *2017 situation report on counterfeiting and piracy in the European Union*, The Hague: Europol and EUIPO.

Europol and Office for Harmonisation in the Internal Market (2016) *2015 situation report on counterfeiting in the European Union*, The Hague: Europol and OHIM.

Falzon, M.A. (2009) *Multi-sited ethnography: Theory, praxis and locality in Contemporary social research*, London: Routledge.

*Financial Times* (2017) 'China mobile payments dwarf those in US as Fintech booms, research shows', *Financial Times*. Available at: https://www.ft.com/content/00585722-ef42-11e6-930f-061b01e23655

Fleming, D.C. (2014) 'Counterfeiting in China', *University of Pennsylvania East Asia Law Review*, 10: 14–35.

*Forbes* (2017) 'How Chinese counterfeiters continue beating Amazon'. Available at: https://www.forbes.com/sites/wadeshepard/2017/01/12/why-amazon-is-losing-its-battle-against-chinese-counterfeiters/#3e4da407585c

Fu, Y. and Hu, X. (2013) 'Cross-border violation of IPR offences and their preventive measures: A case study on a sample of 57 cases in *Yiwu*', *Research on the Rule of Law*, 1: 83–9.

Gambetta, D. (2007) 'Trust's odd ways', in J. Elster, O. Gjelsvik, A. Hylland and K. Moene (eds) *Understanding choice, explaining behaviour: Essays in honour of Ole-Jørgen Skog*, Oslo: Unipub, pp 81–100.

Gessler, C. (2009) *Counterfeiting in the luxury industry*, Saarbrücken: VDM.

Gregson, N. and Crang, M. (2017) 'Illicit economies: customary illegality, moral economies and circulation', *Transactions of the Institute of British Geographers*, 42(2): 206–19.

Guo, J. (2002) 'Several confusing points', *Modern Quality* 3: 36.

Hall, A. and Antonopoulos, G.A. (2015) 'License to pill: Illegal entrepreneurs' tactics in the online trade of medicines', in P.C. van Duyne, A. Maljevic, G.A. Antonopoulos, J. Harvey and K. von Lampe (eds) *The relativity of wrongdoing: Corruption, organised crime, fraud and money laundering in perspective*, Nijmegen: Wolf Legal Publishers, pp 229–52.

Hall, A. and Antonopoulos, G.A. (2016) *Fake meds online: The Internet and the transnational market in illicit pharmaceuticals*, London: Macmillan.

Hall, A. and Antonopoulos, G.A. (2017) '"Coke on tick": Exploring the cocaine market in the UK through the lens of financial management', *Journal of Financial Crime*, 24(2): 181–99.

Hall, A., Koenraadt, R.M. and Antonopoulos, G.A. (2017) 'Illicit pharmaceutical networks in Europe: Organising the illicit medicine market in the United Kingdom and the Netherlands', *Trends in Organised Crime*, DOI: 10.1007/s12117-017-9304-9.

Hall, S. and Winlow, S. (2015) *Revitalizing criminological theory: Towards a new ultra-realism*, London: Routledge.

Hall, S., Winlow, S. and Ancrum, C. (2008) *Criminal identities and consumer culture*, Cullompton: Willan.

Hicks, T. (2015) 'Model approach for investigating the financing of organised crime', policy paper, Centre for the Study of Democracy.

HMRC (Her Majesty's Revenue and Customs) (2004) *Counterfeit cigarettes 2004*, London: HMRC.

HMRC (2014) 'Tea leaf tobacco smugglers sentenced'. Available at: http://www.mynewsdesk.com/uk/hm-revenue-customs-hmrc/news/tea-leaf-tobacco-smugglers-sentenced-92068

Hobbs, D. (1998) 'Going down the glocal: the local context of organised crime', *Howard Journal of Criminal Justice*, 37(4): 407–22.

Hobbs, D. and Antonopoulos, G.A. (2014) 'How to research organised crime', in L. Paoli (ed) *The Oxford handbook of organised crime*, New York, NY: Oxford University Press, pp 96–117.

Hotelling, H. (1929) 'Stability in competition', *Economic Journal*, 39(March): 41–57.

ICC (International Chamber of Commerce) (2011) 'Estimating the global economic and social impacts of counterfeiting and piracy'. Available at: http://www.iccwbo.org/Advocacy-Codes-and-Rules/BASCAP/BASCAP-Research/Economic-impact/Global-Impacts-Study/

Intellectual Property Office (2016) 'Prison time for couple running rake BMW fake accessories'. Available at: https://www.gov.uk/government/news/prison-time-for-couple-running-fake-bmw-accessories-scam

Intellectual Property Office (2017) *Share and share alike: The challenges from social media for intellectual property rights*, Newport: Intellectual Property Office.

Intellectual Property Office and Foreign & Commonwealth Office (2015) 'China–Southeast Asia Anti-Counterfeiting Project summary report'. Available at: https://www.gov.uk/government/uploads/system/uploads/attachment_data/file/482650/China-ASEAN_Anti-Counterfeiting_Project_Report.pdf

International Tax and Investment Centre (no date) *The illicit trade in tobacco products and how to tackle it*, Almaty: International Tax and Investment Centre.

Interpol (2014) 'Against organized crime'. Available at: www.interpol.int

IRACM (International Institute of Research Against Counterfeit Medicines) (2013) *Counterfeit medicines and criminal organizations*, Paris: IRACM.

Junninen, M. (2006) *Adventurers and risk-takers: Finnish professional criminals and their organisations in the 1990s cross-border criminality*, Helsinki: HEUNI.

Kelley, M.B. (2012) 'Counterfeit Chinese microchips are getting so good they can't be identified', *Business Insider*, 16 June.

Kinzig, J. (2004) *Die rechtliche Bewältigung von Erscheinungsformen organisierter Kriminalität*, Berlin: Duncker & Humblot.

Kleemans, E. and De Poot, C. (2008) 'Criminal careers in organised crime and social opportunity structure', *European Journal of Criminology*, 5(1): 69–98.

Kleemans, E. and Van de Bunt, H.G. (2008) 'Organised crime, occupations and opportunity', *Global Crime*, 9(3): 185–97.

Kruisbergen, E.W., Van de Bunt, H.G. and Kleemans, E.R. (2012) *Georganiseerde criminaliteit in Nederland. Vierde rapportage op basis van de Monitor Georganiseerde Criminaliteit*, Den Haag: Boom Juridische Uitgevers.

Laing, B.A. (2005) 'Parallel trade in pharmaceuticals: injecting the counterfeit element into the public health', *NC Journal of International Law and Commercial Regulation*, 31(4): 847–900.

Lan, T. (2015) 'Industrial district and the multiplication of labour: the Chinese apparel industry in Prato, Italy', *Antipode*, 47(1): 158–78.

Lan, T. and Zhu, S. (2015) 'Chinese apparel value chains in Europe: low-end fast fashion, regionalization, and transnational entrepreneurship in Prato, Italy', *Eurasian Geography and Economics*, 55: 156–74.

Large, J. (2015) '"Get real don't buy fakes". Fashion fakes and flawed policy: the problem with taking a consumer-responsibility approach to reducing the problem of counterfeiting', *Criminology and Criminal Justice*, 15(2): 169–85.

Large, J. (forthcoming) *The consumption of counterfeit fashion*, London: Palgrave.

*Legal Daily* (2007) 'Chinese businesses frequently fall into the traps set up by foreign counterfeiters; a sharp increase of IPR cases concerning foreign affairs may connect with overseas criminal groups'. Available at: http://news.sohu.com/20070715/n251060873.shtml

Levi, M. (2004) 'The making of the UK's organised crime control policies', in C. Fijnaut and L. Paoli (eds) *Organised crime in Europe: Concepts, patterns and control policies in the European Union and beyond*, Dordrecht: Springer, pp 823–51.

Levi, M. (2010a) 'Combating the financing of terrorism: a history and assessment of the control of "threat finance"', *British Journal of Criminology* (Special Issue Terrorism: Criminological Perspectives), 50(4): 650–69.

Levi, M. (2010b) 'Proceeds of crime: fighting the financing of terrorism', *Criminal Justice Matters*, 81(1): 38–9.

Levi, M. (2013) *Drug law enforcement and financial investigation practices*, London: IDPC.

L'Hoiry, X. (2013) '"Shifting the stuff wasn't any bother" – illicit enterprise, tobacco bootlegging and deconstructing the British government's cigarette smuggling discourse', *Trends in Organised Crime*, 16: 413–34.

Li, L. (2007) 'Are Chinese counterfeits travelling around the world?', *Finance and Economics*, 21: 21–3.

Lin, Y.J. (2011) *Fake stuff: China and the rise of counterfeit goods*, London: Routledge.

Local Government Association (2015) *Tackling serious and organised crime: A local response*, London: Local Government Association.

Lord, N., Spencer, J., Bellotti, E. and Benson, K. (2017) 'A script analysis of the distribution of counterfeit alcohol across two European jurisdictions', *Trends in Organised Crime*, DOI: 10.1007/s12117-017-9305-8.

Makowski, L. and Ostroy, J.M. (2001) 'Perfect competition and the creativity of the market', *Journal of Economic Literature*, 39: 479–535.

Maskus, K.E. (2001) 'Parallel imports in pharmaceuticals: implications for competition and prices in developing counties', final report to the World Intellectual Property Organisation.

Mathews, G. (2007) 'Chungking mansions: a center of "low-end globalization"', *Ethnology*, 46(2): 169–83.

Mathews, G., Lin, D. and Yang, Y. (2014) 'How to evade states and slip past borders: lessons from traders, overstayers, and asylum seekers in Hong Kong and China', *City & Society*, 26(2): 217–38.

Mills, H., Skodbo, S. and Blyth, P. (2013) *Understanding organised crime: Estimating the scale and the social and economic costs*, Research report 73, London: Home Office.

Moeller, K. (2012) 'Costs and revenues in street level cannabis dealing', *Trends in Organised Crime*, 15(1): 31–46.

Moneyval (2005) *Proceeds from trafficking in human beings and illegal migration*, Strasbourg: Council of Europe.

Morselli, C. and Roy, J. (2008) 'Brokerage qualifications in ringing operations', *Criminology*, 46(1): 71–98.

*Nanfang Metropolis Daily* (2015) 'Guangzhou police raided a counterfeiting workshop: perfumes were made of fragrant essences and purified water'. Available at: http://www.oeeee.com/nis/201506/15/361537.html

*National Business Daily* (2015) 'Unveiling highly imitated designer bags'. Available at: http://www.nbd.com.cn/articles/2015-03-23/904891.html

Navarrete, M. (2015) 'Europol's role in countering criminal finances', presentation at the Dutch Ministry of Security and Justice, The Hague, March.

Naylor, R.T. (1996) 'From underworld to underground: enterprise crime, "informal sector" business, and the public policy', *Crime, Law and Social Change*, 24: 79–150.

Naylor, R.T. (2004) *Wages of crime*, Ithaca, NY: Cornell University Press.

OECD (Organisation for Economic Co-operation and Development) (2017) *Trade in counterfeit ICT goods*, Paris: OECD.

OECD and EUIPO (European Union Intellectual Property Office) (2016) *Trade in counterfeit and pirated goods*, Paris: OECD.

OECD and EUIPO (2017) *Mapping the real routes in trade of fake goods*, Paris: OECD.

Office for Harmonisation in the Internal Market (2014) '2014 situation report on counterfeiting in the European Union'. Available at: https://oami.europa.eu/ohimportal/documents/11370/80606/2014+Situation+Report+on+Counterfeiting+in+the+EU

Office for Harmonisation in the Internal Market (2015) '2015 situation report on counterfeiting in the European Union'. Available at: https://oami.europa.eu/ohimportal/documents/11370/80606/2015+Situation+Report+on+Counterfeiting+in+the+EU

OLAF (*Office Européen de Lutte Anti-Fraude* [European Anti-Fraud Office]) (2012) *Illicit tobacco trade*, Paris: OLAF.

Pang, L. (2008) '"China who makes and fakes": a semiotics of the counterfeit', *Theory, Culture & Society*, 25(6): 117–40.

Passas, N. (2005) *Informal value transfer systems and criminal activities*, Den Haag: WODC.

Petrunov, G. (2011) 'Managing money acquired from human trafficking', *Trends in Organised Crime*, 14: 165–83.

Qian, J. (2008) 'Original Equipment Manufacture (OEM) and the infringements of trademark rights', *Journal of Zhejiang University of Technology (Social Science)*, 7(4): 474–80.

Reuter, P. (1985) *The organisation of illegal markets*, Washington, DC: National Institute of Justice.

Reuter, P. (2013) 'Are estimates of money laundering volume either feasible or useful?', in B. Unger and D. van der Linden (eds) *Handbook on money laundering*, Cheltenham: Elgar, pp 224–31.

Reuter, P.,MacCoun, R. andMurphy, P. (1990) *Money from crime*,Washington, DC: RAND.

*Reuters* (2017) 'How China's biggest bank became ensnared in a sprawling money laundering probe: Angus Berwick and David Lague', 31 July. Available at: http://www.reuters.com/investigates/special-report/icbc-spain/

Rojek, C. (2017) 'Counterfeit commerce: relations of production, distribution and exchange', *Cultural Sociology*, 11(1): 28–43.

Sassen, S. (1998) *Globalisation and its discontents: Essays on the new mobility of people and money*, New York, NY: The New Press.

Satchwell, G. (2004) *A sick business: Counterfeit medicines and organised crime*, London: The Stockholm Network.

Schneider, F. (2012) 'The hidden financial flows of the organized crime: a literature review and some preliminary empirical results', in C.C. Storti and P. de Grauwe (eds) *Illicit trade and the global economy*, Boston, MA: The MIT Press, pp 31–45.

Schneider, F. (2016) 'The financial flows of transnational crime and tax fraud in OECD countries', in G.A. Antonopoulos (ed) *Illegal entrepreneurship, organised crime and social control*, New York, NY: Springer, pp 143–59.

Sezneva, O. (2012) 'The pirates of Nevskii Prospekt: intellectual property, piracy and institutional diffusion in Russia', *Poetics*, 40(2): 150–66.

Shen, A. (2017) '"Being affluent, one drinks wine": wine counterfeiting in mainland China', paper presented at Crime and Justice in Asia and the Global South, Cairns, Australia, July.

Shen, A. and Antonopoulos, G.A. (2016) '"No banquet can do without liquor": alcohol counterfeiting in the People's Republic in China', *Trends in Organised Crime*, DOI: 10.1007/s12117-016-9296-x.

Shen, A., Antonopoulos, G.A. and Von Lampe, K. (2010) '"The dragon breathes smoke": cigarette counterfeiting in the People's Republic of China', *British Journal of Criminology*, 50(2): 239–58.

Shen, A., Antonopoulos, G.A., Kurti, M. and Von Lampe, K. (2012) 'The neoliberal wings of the smoke-breathing dragon: the cigarette counterfeiting business and economic development in China', in P. Whitehead and P. Crawshaw (eds) *Organising neoliberalism: Markets, privatisation and justice*, London: Anthem Press, pp 81–104.

Silke, A. (2000) 'Drink, drugs and rock'n'roll: financing loyalist terrorism in Northern Ireland – part two', *Studies in Conflict and Terrorism*, 23(2): 107–27.

Simmel, G. (2004) *The philosophy of money*, London: Psychology Press.

Skinnari, J. (2010) 'The financial management of drug crime in Sweden', in P.C. van Duyne, G.A. Antonopoulos, J. Harvey, A. Maljevic, T. Vander Beken and K. von Lampe (eds) *Cross-border crime inroads on integrity in Europe*, Nijmegen: WLP, pp 189–215.

Soudijn, M.R.J. and Zegers, B.C.H. (2012) 'Cyber-crime and virtual offender convergence', *Trends in Organised Crime*, 15(2/3): 111–29.

Soudijn, M.R.J. and Zhang, S.X. (2013) 'Taking loansharking into account: a case study of Chinese vest-pocket lenders in Holland', *Trends in Organised Crime*, 16: 13–30.

Southwick, N. (2013) 'Counterfeit drugs kill 1 mn people annually: Interpol', *InSight Crime*, 24 October, Available at: http://www.insightcrime.org/news-briefs/counterfeit-drugs-kill-1-million-annually-interpol

Spapens, T. (2017) 'Cannabis cultivation in the Tilburg area: how much money is involved and where does it go?', in P.C. van Duyne, J. Harvey, G.A. Antonopoulos and K. von Lampe (eds) *The many faces of crime for profit and ways of tackling it*, Nijmegen: Wolf Legal Publishers, pp 219–41.

Statista (2017) 'Online payment in China'. Available at: https://www.statista.com/topics/1211/online-payment-in-china/

Stoller, P. (2002) *Money has no smell: The Africanisation of New York City*, Chicago, IL: University of Chicago Press.

Sullivan, B.A. and Wilson, J.M. (2016) 'An empirical examination of product counterfeiting crime impacting the U.S. military', *Trends in Organised Crime*, DOI: 10.1007/s12117-017-9306-7.

*The Gazette* (2016) 'Ciggie smugglers gambled away cash', *The Gazette*, 3 December.

*The Guardian* (2013) 'UK sees sixfold increase in seizure of counterfeit electrical goods', *The Guardian*, 29 March. Available at: http://www.guardian.co.uk/uk/2013/mar/29/uk-seizure-counterfeit-electrical-goods?INTCMP=SRCH

*The Guardian* (2014) 'Counterfeit traders fuelling demand for cheap and potentially dangerous booze', *The Guardian*, 10 June. Available at: https://www.theguardian.com/society/2014/jun/10/counterfeit-traders-demand-cheap-booze

The Scottish Government (2016) *Scotland's serious organised crime strategy – 2016 annual report*, Edinburgh: The Scottish Government.

Thomas, D. (2003) *An underworld at war*, London: Murray.

Tilley, N. and Hopkins, M. (2008) 'Organised crime and local business', *Criminology and Criminal Justice*, 8(4): 443–59.

Transcrime (2013) *The factbook on the illicit trade in tobacco products: Issue 1 – United Kingdom*, Milan: Transcrime.

Treadwell, J. (2011) 'From the car book to booting it up? eBay, online counterfeit crime and the transformation of the criminal marketplace', *Criminal & Criminal Justice*, 12(2): 175–91.

Union des Fabricants (2003) *Counterfeiting and organised crime*, Paris: Union des Fabricants.

Union des Fabricants (2016) *Counterfeiting and terrorism*, Paris: Union des Fabricants.

UNODC (United Nations Office on Drugs and Crime) (no date) 'The illicit trafficking of counterfeit goods and transnational organised crime'. Available at: https://www.unodc.org/documents/counterfeit/FocusSheet/Counterfeit_focussheet_EN_HIRES.pdf

UNODC (2010) *The globalisation of crime: A transnational organised crime threat assessment*, Vienna: UNODC.

UNODC (2015) *The illicit trafficking in counterfeit goods and transnational organised crime*, Vienna: UNODC.

Valenzuela, A. (2001) 'Day labourers as entrepreneurs?', *Journal of Ethnic and Migration Studies*, 27(2): 335–52.

Van de Bunt, H.G. and Kleemans, E. (2007) 'Organised crime in The Netherlands: third report of the organized crime monitor' (English summary). Available at: https://english.wodc.nl/binaries/ob252_summary_tcm29-66835.pdf

Van Duyne, P.C. (2000) 'Mobsters are human too: behavioural science and organised crime investigation', *Crime, Law & Social Change*, 34(4): 369–90.

Van Duyne, P.C. (2007) 'Criminal finances and state of the art: case for concern?', in P.C. van Duyne, A. Maljevic, M. van Dijck, K. von Lampe and J. Harvey (eds) *Crime business and crime money in Europe: The dirty linen of illicit enterprise*, Nijmegen: Wolf Legal Publishers, pp 69–95.

Van Duyne, P.C. and Levi, M. (2005) *Drugs and money*, London: Routledge.

Van Duyne, P.C. and Soudijn, M. (2010) 'Crime-money in the financial system', in M. Herzog-Evans (ed) *Transnational criminology*, Nijmegen: WLP.

Van Duyne, P.C., De Zanger, W. and Kristen, F. (2014) 'Greedy of crime money', in P.C. van Duyne, J. Harvey, G.A. Antonopoulos, K. von Lampe, A. Maljevic and A. Markovska (eds) *Corruption, greed and crime money*, Nijmgen: WLP, pp 235–66.

Von Lampe, K. (2007) 'Criminals are not alone: some observations on the social microcosm of illegal entrepreneurs', in P.C. van Duyne, A. Maljevic, M. van Dijck, K. von Lampe and J. Harvey (eds) *Crime business and crime money in Europe: The dirty linen of illicit enterprise*, Nijmegen: Wolf Legal Publishers, pp 131–55.

Von Lampe, K. (2016) *Organised crime*, Los Angeles, CA: Sage.

Von Lampe, K. and Johansen, P.O. (2004) 'Organised crime and trust', *Global Crime*, 6: 159–84.

Wagner, W.J. (no date) *Cross-border trade in pharmaceuticals: Free trade or illegal trade*, Ottawa, ON: Gowlings.

Walker, T. (2014) 'FedEx facing drug-trafficking charges over illicit pharmaceuticals', *The Independent*, 20 July.

Wall, D.S. and Large, J. (2010) 'Jailhouse frocks: Locating the public interest in policing intellectual property crime', *British Journal of Criminology*, 50(6): 1094–116.

Wang, N. (2014) 'Trademark issues in regard to international OEM in China and countermeasures', *Academic Exploration*, 1(1): 49–93.

Winlow, S. (2001) *Badfellas*, Oxford: Berg.

World Economic Forum (2015) 'State of the illicit economy'. Available at: http://www3.weforum.org/docs/WEF_State_of_the_Illicit_Economy_2015_2.pdf

*Xinhua News* (2016) 'Guangdong detected 64 counterfeiting cases in the first 8 months, taking half of the total number of counterfeiting cases in China'. Available at: http://www.gd.xinhuanet.com/newscenter/2016-09/29/c_1119648501.htm

*Xinjing Bao* (2014) 'University student made 2 million in 2 years by selling counterfeits'. Available at: http://tech.caijing.com.cn/2014-01-06/113776646.html

*Yangtse Wanbao* (2017) 'Counterfeit top-end cosmetics, including Jo Malone, sold online were made next to a toilet'. Available at: http://www.yangtse.com/m/news/jiangsu/nanjing/2017-04-20/416222.htm

Yar, M. (2005) 'A deadly faith in fakes: Trademark theft and the global trade in counterfeit automotive parts', *Internet Journal of Criminology*. Available at: http://www.internetjournalofcriminology.com

Ye, B. (2000) 'Grasp the new characteristics of the counterfeiting business; take corresponding measures to succeed', *City Technique Supervision*, 4: 12–13.

Zelizer, V.A. (1989) 'The social meaning of money: "special monies"', *The American Journal of Sociology*, 95: 342–77.

Zelizer, V.A. (2011) *Economic lives: How culture shapes the economy*, Princeton, NJ: Princeton University Press.

Zhao, Z. and Xu, J. (2009) 'Revival of small and medium enterprises in China will take a little while'. Available at: http://news.sina.com.cn/o/2009-05-28/033915696160s.shtml

# Index